INSIDE FORENSIC SCIENCE

Forensic DNA Analysis

INSIDE FORENSIC SCIENCE

Forensic DNA Analysis

Lawrence Kobilinsky, Ph.D.,
Louis Levine, Ph.D., and
Henrietta Margolis-Nunno, Ph.D., J.D.

SERIES EDITOR | Lawrence Kobilinsky, Ph.D.

CHELSEA HOUSE
PUBLISHERS
An imprint of Infobase Publishing

Forensic DNA Analysis

Chelsea House
An imprint of Infobase Publishing
132 West 31st Street
New York NY 10001

ISBN-10: 0-7910-8923-1
ISBN-13: 978-0-7910-8923-1

Library of Congress Cataloging-in-Publication Data

Kobilinsky, Lawrence
 Forensic DNA analysis / Lawrence Kobilinsky, Louis Levine,
 Henrietta Margolis-Nunno.
    p. cm. — (Inside forensic science)
 Includes bibliographical references and index.
 ISBN 0-7910-8923-1 (hardcover)
 1. DNA Analysis. 2. Forensic genetics. 3. Forensic pathology. I. Levine, Louis. II.
 Margolis-Nunno, Henrietta. III. Title. IV. Series.
 RA1057.55K63 2006
 614'.1—dc22   2006025586

Chelsea House books are available at special discounts when purchased in bulk quantities for businesses, associations, institutions, or sales promotions. Please call our Special Sales Department in New York at (212) 967-8800 or (800) 322-8755.

You can find Chelsea House on the World Wide Web at http://www.chelseahouse.com

Text design by Annie O'Donnell
Cover design by Ben Peterson

Printed in the United States of America

Bang FOF 10 9 8 7 6 5 4 3 2 1

This book is printed on acid-free paper.

All links and Web addresses were checked and verified to be correct at the time of publication. Because of the dynamic nature of the Web, some addresses and links may have changed since publication and may no longer be valid.

Table of Contents

How to Identify a Criminal

The problem of identifying a criminal who commits a crime and escapes without being seen is all too common in human history. One example of such an event can be found in the Old Testament, which tells the story of the rivalry between Cain and Abel (the sons of Adam and Eve) and Abel's murder by Cain. When God asks where Abel is, Cain tries to avoid the question by replying: "Am I my brother's keeper?" God's well-known accusation follows: "The blood of your brother cries out to me, from the ground." The biblical reference to "blood" as the evidence identifying the criminal is fascinating; the analysis of blood has been and continues to be one of the more reliable methods used in solving crimes.

Other methods of identifying guilty individuals are found in the folklore of a number of ethnic groups. A Chinese chronicle tells of two farmers who argued in a field. Using his sickle, one farmer killed the other and then fled the scene unobserved. Later he wiped the bloodstains from his sickle as best he could. The wise men of the village assembled all the farmers and had each one place his sickle on the ground. In a few minutes, attracted to the very small specks of blood that the farmer had overlooked, flies began to gather on the murder weapon. Confronted with such convincing evidence, the sickle's owner confessed to the crime.

A story from the Bedouin tribes of North Africa describes a different approach, involving self-incrimination. A suspect is brought to a darkened tent containing a donkey. The individual is made to believe that the animal has special powers when it is in the dark, namely that it will emit a loud cry if a person guilty of a crime pulls its tail, but it will remain silent if he is innocent. The suspect is told to enter the tent alone, locate the faintly visible donkey, and pull its tail. Unknown to the suspect, black oil has been applied to the animal's tail. Also unknown to him is the fact that a donkey will not cry out when its tail is pulled. An examination of the person's hands, when he emerges from the tent, indicates whether or not he has pulled the donkey's tail. If his hands are stained with oil, it shows that he has pulled the animal's tail, something only an innocent person would do. Clean hands, however, reveal the suspect's guilt.

In modern times, the techniques of gathering evidence have changed, but the problem of identifying an unknown criminal remains the same. It is important to note that every properly conducted crime scene investigation rests on a single principle put forth in 1910 by French criminologist Edmond Locard: "Every contact leaves a trace." He was convinced that, whenever a crime is committed, evidence is transferred between the criminal and the crime scene (for example, the victim, furniture, carpets, glassware, windows, doors). This concept is referred to as **Locard's Exchange Principle.** The evidence can be a fingerprint of the criminal on a window or door, a strand of the criminal's hair under the victim's fingernail, a thread from a victim's sweater on the clothing of the criminal, or a drop of the victim's blood that dripped onto the criminal's body during a violent struggle. It is clear that only diligent and painstaking examination will result in the collection of all the evidence there is to be found.

Although this book emphasizes the role of DNA in solving crimes, it is important to briefly examine the place of fingerprints in identifying an individual. It is unknown when and by whom it was first recognized that each person has a unique set of fingerprints. It is known, however, that in 1870 William Herschel, who was chief colonial administrative officer of Bengal, India, used thumbprints to confirm the identity of his workers, many of whom could neither read nor write. On being paid their wages, the workers were required to dip their thumbs into a dish containing ink and then place their prints on the payroll next to the amount paid. This was done to discourage a second request for payment later. It is interesting to note that the first use of thumbprints was not to solve a crime but to prevent one from taking place.

Fingerprints were not immediately accepted as evidence in criminal cases. Starting in 1911, however, after a good deal of scientific investigation and despite challenges by defense attorneys in various trials, fingerprints were accepted as valid indicators of an individual's presence at a crime scene.

The next significant advance in placing a suspect at a particular place was the ability to establish the presence of one or more of the suspect's body tissues (for example, skin, hair, blood, or nail clippings) at the site of the investigation. It was quickly realized that blood was the tissue most often found. A laboratory procedure was developed to establish that the specimen was (1) blood rather than a chemical dye, and (2) human blood rather than that of some animal.

Blood consists of two parts: cells and plasma. Many **traits** of blood cells are useful in identifying individuals. The traits that were most helpful in forensics, prior to the early 1990s, are those characterizing the surfaces of the blood cells. Among the many such traits, the most used has been the system consisting of the A, B, O, and AB blood types. Discovered by Karl Landsteiner in 1900, these blood types are crucial in determining which blood transfusions will be successful and which will result in the recipient's illness or death. In addition, these blood types are an important component of the evidence linking a suspect to a crime. Information about the pattern of inheritance of blood types is also used to help determine paternity and maternity in parentage disputes. It is important to point out that this advance in individual identification, in effect, established the field of genetic evidence.

GENETIC EVIDENCE

When and how did the development of the field of genetic evidence become possible? Again, 1900 is the significant year. It was then that other scientists confirmed Gregor Mendel's experimental findings on the inheritance of traits. Applying Mendel's findings to human beings, we can see that each of us is a result of the fusion of a sperm, carrying 23 **chromosomes**, with an egg, which also carries 23 chromosomes. Based on decreasing size, the chromosomes in both egg and sperm are numbered 1 to 22, with the first chromosome being the longest (Figure 1.1). The last chromosome is the one that determines sex: An individual is either XY (male) or XX (female). The 22 **autosomes**—the chromosomes that do not determine gender—are matched for size, and the **genes** in each pair of matched (**homologous**) chromosomes determine the same traits of the individual. They are, therefore, referred to as homologous genes.

Homologous genes may be identical or different. Where studies show that a gene for a given trait has different forms, each form is called an **allele**. A person who carries identical alleles for a trait is referred to as a **homozygote** for that trait; an

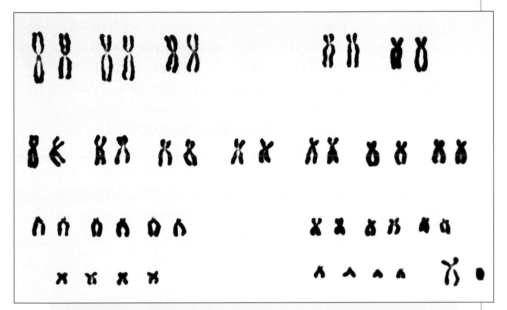

FIGURE 1.1 A complete set of 46 chromosomes of a cell from a male is arranged in homologous pairs. The Y chromosome is located in the bottom right corner of the photograph. To the left of the Y chromosome is the X chromosome. A comparable figure from a female cell would differ only in the absence of the Y chromosome and the presence of a second X chromosome.

individual who carries different alleles for a trait is referred to as a **heterozygote** for the trait. The characteristic appearance (physical, or behavioral) of the trait is called its **phenotype**; the underlying allelic composition producing the trait is called its **genotype**. Through a study of a family's **pedigree,** one can, in most cases, establish the genetic basis for the inheritance of a particular trait.

Returning to the A, B, O, and AB blood types, studies of many family lines led to the conclusion that a gene for this blood cell characteristic is located on each of our homologous number 9 chromosomes. Further, depending on the family line, each gene can have one of three alleles, called A, B, and O. The alleles also have interesting relationships to one another. If an individual has the genotype AA or AO, the phenotype will be blood type A; that is, A dominates O. If the genotype is BB or BO, the phenotype will be blood type B (B dominates O). If the individual's genotype is AB, however, the phenotype will also be AB because both alleles are expressed. The genotype OO results in the phenotype O.

As with fingerprints, blood-type genetic evidence was challenged when it was first introduced in court cases. One of the more high-profile examples of this occurred in 1946, in the case of *Barry v. Chaplin*. Charlie Chaplin, star of silent films, became a director in his later years and promoted the careers of a number of young actresses. Joan Barry was one of them. During the course of their relationship, Barry became pregnant. After the birth of a child, she sued Chaplin for support of the child.

An A, B, O, AB blood-type test was performed. Barry was found to be blood type A, which meant her genotype could be either AA or AO. If she was AA, all her eggs would carry the A allele. If she was AO, any egg she produced could carry either the A or the O allele. Chaplin was found to be blood type O, which meant that he was OO in genotype, and all his sperm must carry the O allele. The child was found to be AB, eliminating Chaplin as the biological father.

The jury chose to ignore the genetic evidence, however, and, influenced by testimony detailing Chaplin's romantic relationship with Barry, ordered Chaplin to support the child. Contrary to his attorney's advice, Chaplin chose not to appeal the case and supported the child until adulthood. The source of the B-allele-carrying sperm remains unknown.

Soon after the discovery of the A, B, O, and AB blood types, other blood-group systems were found. Today, at least 23 blood-group systems are known that can potentially aid in solving crimes. A shortcoming of this or any system that derives genotype from phenotype, however, is the possibility that a very slight difference in genotype might not be reflected in phenotype. In effect, the only way we can be certain about an individual's genotype is by analyzing the chemical composition of the person's genetic material, namely, his or her DNA.

As often happens in science, the basic discovery that opened the field of DNA research and study occurred many years before the field was actually developed. In 1871, Friedrich Miescher published a method for separating cell nuclei from cytoplasm. From these cell nuclei, he extracted an acid material he called **nuclein**, which differed in chemical composition from the carbohydrates, lipids, and proteins normally found in cells. Later called **nucleic acid**, nuclein was found to occur in two forms: (1) **deoxyribonucleic acid (DNA)** and (2) **ribonucleic acid (RNA).** The DNA was subsequently shown to be the genetic material of all cellular forms and all but a few strains of viruses, which instead have RNA. In cellular forms, RNA functions in the **translation** of the DNA genetic blueprint into the organism's phenotype. In some traits (for example, human adult height), the phenotypic expression of the genotype varies depending on such environmental factors as the nutrition and illnesses of the person during early life. In other traits (for example, A, B, O, and AB blood types), phenotype does not depend on environmental factors.

THE STRUCTURE OF DNA

In 1953, nearly a century after the discovery of nucleic acid, James Watson and Francis Crick published their now-famous paper in the British scientific journal *Nature*, presenting a three-dimensional model of the structure of DNA (Figure 1.2). They found it had an elegantly simple architecture, consisting of two parallel chains of compounds called **nucleotides** that formed a shape called a double-helix running the length of

FIGURE 1.2 James Watson *(left)* and Francis Crick *(right)* are pictured with their model of DNA created in 1951. Watson, Crick, and a third scientist, Maurice Wilkins, shared the 1962 Nobel Prize for Physiology or Medicine for their elucidation of the structure of DNA.

each chromosome. Later research found that a set of 23 human chromosomes has about 3.1 billion nucleotide pairs.

Knowing the configuration of DNA does not give us the DNA evidence that investigators need to solve a crime. We have to be able to isolate and identify specific sections of the DNA that can be used to provide genetic profiles of the suspect and the evidence. Historically, there have been two solutions to this problem. The first originated in 1964, when Werner Arber isolated so-called **restriction enzymes** from bacteria. In bacteria, these enzymes, of which there are many, serve to cut the DNA of the DNA-containing viruses that would otherwise invade and kill the bacteria. By cutting the viral DNA into many small sections, the enzymes destroy the viruses. Not until 21 years later, however, in 1985, did Alec Jeffreys, working with these restriction enzymes, cut human DNA into many different-sized sections. He further found that the sections obtained from an individual were common to that person's family line and could be used in parentage disputes.

DNA AS EVIDENCE

The first use of DNA evidence to settle a legal problem involved an immigration dispute. A boy from Ghana tried to enter the United Kingdom to join his mother, who had been living there for some time. A problem arose when the boy could not present any documentation to prove that he was in fact her son. The situation was complicated by the fact that the boy's father was not available. A DNA study of the boy, his mother, brother, and two sisters showed that all of the children had the same father and that the boy was indeed the mother's son. Unfortunately, the procedure used, called **restriction fragment length polymorphism (RFLP)**, is extremely laborious, and the sections of DNA obtained are actually "clusters" of similarly sized DNA segments that are positioned next to each other and known as **variable number of tandem repeats (VNTRs)**. The "identifying number" assigned to a VNTR is, in fact, the average size of the slightly different DNA segments a particular cluster contains. With the advent of a simpler, more precise method of obtaining and analyzing DNA, the FBI and other crime laboratories discontinued the use of RFLP.

Another unrelated advance in obtaining DNA evidence was also made in 1985, when Kary Mullis devised a procedure to multiply particular sections of DNA. Starting with the DNA from about 150 cells, he could produce more than one billion copies of any desired DNA section. The procedure became known as the **polymerase chain reaction** (PCR). For comparison purposes, note that a bloodstain the size of the period at the end of this sentence contains sufficient DNA for the PCR procedure, but RFLP would need a bloodstain the size of a dime. In addition, each DNA section used in PCR consists of some number of sets of four nucleotides (**tetranucleotides**). The identifying number assigned to each DNA section, referred to as a **short tandem repeat (STR),** is the actual number of tetranucleotide sets contained in that STR. The ability to use actual numbers (STRs) rather than averages (VNTRs) makes comparing evidence and suspect DNA more accurate and meaningful.

Although the science of identifying criminals will undoubtedly continue to advance, it is important to note that, in the year 2000, the FBI and other laboratories stopped using RFLP and switched to PCR-based methods for all their analyses of DNA evidence.

DNA: Sources and Structure

2

As stated in the previous chapter, DNA is the genetic blueprint of an individual. It is present in every cell of a person's body, not only in the cell's **nucleus** but also in its cytoplasm, in special energy-producing structures called *mitochondria.* Of great importance is the fact that, except for the rare occurrence of a **mutation**, the DNA in every cell of the person's body is identical. As a result, DNA can be taken from saliva, blood, skin cells, sweat, bone cells, or hair for individual identification. Body fluids containing cells are often collected as biological evidence. In the case of saliva, the cells are derived from the inner lining of the person's cheek; in sweat, the cells come from the tissue surrounding the sweat glands and pores. In addition to these sources of DNA, one must add semen in the case of a male and breast milk in the case of a female individual.

The many opportunities to obtain DNA evidence can be seen, for example, in the number of places where saliva has been identified: a bite mark, an area licked, bed linens, a mask worn, paper tissue, a washcloth, a cigarette butt, a toothpick, the rim of a bottle or can, and even dental floss. DNA evidence can also be collected from fingernail scrapings, the inside and outside sur-

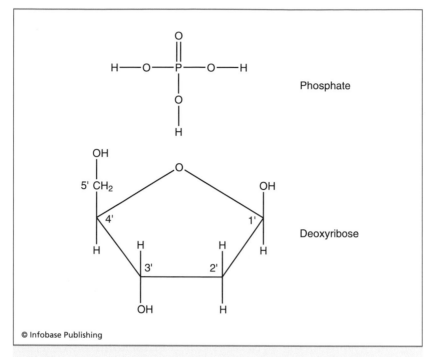

FIGURE 2.1   The chemical structure of a phosphate molecule and the structure of the sugar deoxyribose, two components of DNA, are shown here.

faces of a used condom, clothing, adhesive tape, a vaginal swab, an anal swab, and an oral swab.

DNA STRUCTURE

DNA consists of two parallel spiral strands that form a double-helix. Each strand is actually a linked chain in which the links consist of a very large number of units called nucleotides. Every nucleotide is made up of three smaller chemical compounds: (1) a phosphate, (2) a sugar, and (3) a base (Figures 2.1 and 2.2). There are four different bases, which are referred to by the first letter of their names: A (**adenine**), T (**thymine**), G (**guanine**),

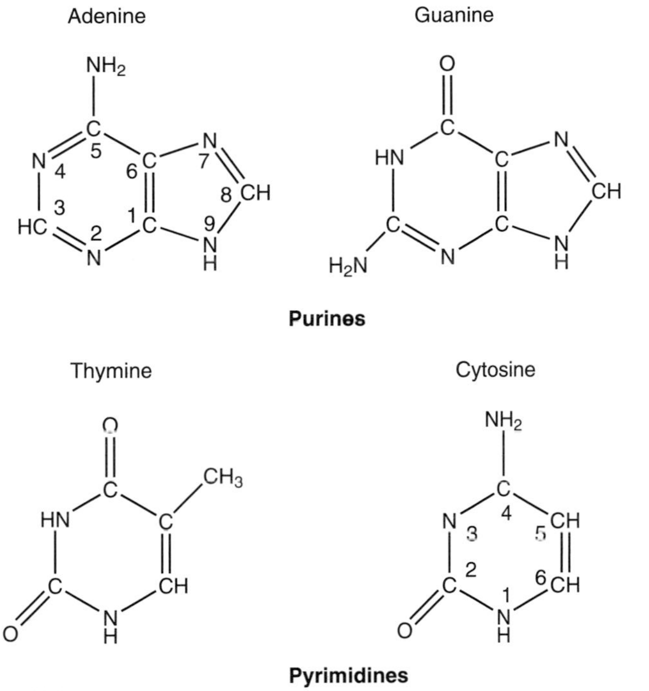

FIGURE 2.2 The chemical structures of the bases in DNA are shown here.

and C (**cytosine**). A and G are double-ringed nitrogen-containing compounds, called **purines**; T and C are single-ringed nitrogen-containing compounds, called **pyrimidines**. The base is the important identifying part of a nucleotide.

Each phosphate group is linked to a sugar molecule, which, in turn, is attached to one of the four nitrogen-containing bases. The phosphate group of each nucleotide is, with one exception in each strand, also chemically bonded to the sugar molecule of the adjacent nucleotide, forming the **polynucleotide chain**. The exceptions are the uppermost phosphate molecule of the "a" (left) strand and the lowermost phosphate molecule of the "b" (right) strand, which are each attached to only one sugar molecule. The location of the singly attached phosphate molecule of each chain establishes a linear orientation, called **polarity**, on that polynucleotide strand. Thus, the DNA molecule consists of two spiraling

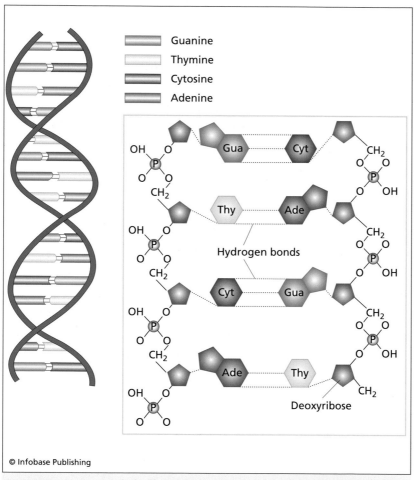

Guanine
Thymine
Cytosine
Adenine

Hydrogen bonds

Deoxyribose

© Infobase Publishing

FIGURE 2.3 The structure of DNA resembles a ladder that has been twisted around itself. The rungs of the ladder are composed of the four nucleotide bases: guanine (G), cytosine (C), adenine (A), and thymine (T). Each nucleotide always bonds with its complementary base pair; guanine bonds with cytosine, while adenine bonds with thymine.

strands oriented in **antiparallel** fashion. All chemical reactions involving the nucleotides of the left chain will proceed from top to bottom; the reverse is true for the right-hand strand.

The positions of the bases in the two strands of DNA are fixed, such that an A in one chain is always attached to a T in the other chain, and correspondingly, a G is always joined to a C, forming complementary **base pairs** (Figure 2.3). The base of one nucleotide is attached to the base of its complement through the action of weak chemical bonds known as **hydrogen bonds**. Two hydrogen bonds always connect an A with a T, and three hydrogen bonds connect a G with a C. The arrangement by which a purine is always linked to a pyrimidine results in a double helix with a uniform diameter. This cylindrical molecule contains major and minor grooves that may be related to its function.

NUCLEAR AND MITOCHONDRIAL DNA

Although DNA in the nuclear chromosome and the cytoplasmic mitochondria of a cell are composed of complementary polynucleotide chains, their numbers, sizes, and geometric arrangements are quite different. As you will recall, a typical cell has 46 or, more technically, 23 pairs of chromosomes, having received one of every pair of homologous chromosomes from each parent. About 3.1 billion base pairs in the total complement of nucleotides are present in a set of 23 chromosomes. The number varies slightly depending on whether the set of chromosomes being considered includes the X, resulting in more base pairs, or the Y chromosome. By contrast, the number of mitochondria varies greatly with the type of cell and stage of its development, ranging usually between 200 and 1,000; the number of nucleotides in a mitochondrial DNA molecule is fixed at 16,569 base pairs.

Within each nuclear chromosome, for most of the **cell cycle**, is only one DNA molecule (in its double-helical construction)

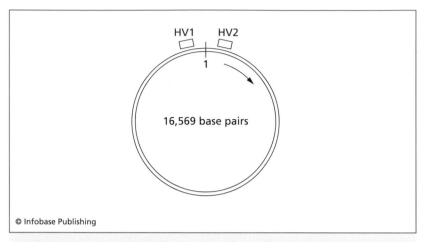

FIGURE 2.4   This diagram of a mitochondrial DNA chromosome shows the location of the subdivisions (HV1 and HV2) of the control region.

running the length of the chromosome. Each mitochondrion, however, typically contains two or three DNA molecules. Furthermore, the ends of each mitochondrial DNA molecule are bonded together, forming a total of two or three circular DNA rings per mitochondrion. By common agreement, the ring chromosome is viewed as the face of a clock with the base pairs numbered from 1 at the 12 o'clock position and proceeding clockwise to 16,569.

Nuclear and mitochondrial chromosomes consist of two types of nucleotides: (1) those that make up the genes, called **coding sequences**, and (2) those whose function is largely unknown, referred to as **noncoding regions**. The nucleotides in coding and noncoding portions of a chromosome are exactly alike in chemical composition and bonding characteristics; they differ solely in whether or not they contribute to one or more of the individual's traits (phenotype).

In nuclear chromosomes, the coding and noncoding sequences are distributed intermittently along the length of each DNA double helix. In a mitochondrial ring chromosome, the coding and noncoding areas are entirely separate, with the noncoding portion of the chromosome being located in a region referred to as the **control region** (also called the displacement loop or **D-loop**). The control region contains about 1,100 base pairs and is divided into 2 distinct sections, hypervariable 1 (HV1) and hypervariable 2 (HV2), as shown in Figure 2.4. The various base sequences of the control region nucleotides are the most useful in identifying an unknown criminal, a partially decomposed body, the parents of kidnapped children, or the body parts from a mass disaster.

Finally, the nuclear chromosomes and cytoplasmic mitochondria are transferred from one generation to the next along different paths, which greatly affects their applications in forensic situations, as we will discuss in the next chapter.

3

The Genetics Underlying Forensic DNA Typing

All organisms are composed of cells. Most of a cell's DNA is found in its nucleus (plural, nuclei), wrapped around proteins, and organized into tightly coiled units called chromosomes. Genes are segments of DNA that usually control traits and are passed from generation to generation.

In humans, sperm or egg (**ovum**; plural, ova) cells are called **gametes**, and each contains 23 chromosomes. All other cells, called **somatic cells**, contain 46 chromosomes—2 **sex chromosomes** and 22 pairs of autosomes (nonsex chromosomes). The sex chromosomes (X and Y) determine the sex (or gender) of an individual; human males have an X and a Y chromosome (XY) and females have a pair of X chromosomes (XX). A set of genes found on the Y chromosome, called SRY (sex-determining region of the Y chromosome), determines if an embryo will develop into a male or female. Each chromosome in the pair of autosomes comes from a different parent, and the pair is homologous because it carries the genes for the same traits and has a similar appearance under a microscope. Thus, the 46 chromosomes of a somatic cell can be thought of as two sets of 23, and these cells are said to be **diploid**. Sperm and egg cells contain only one set of

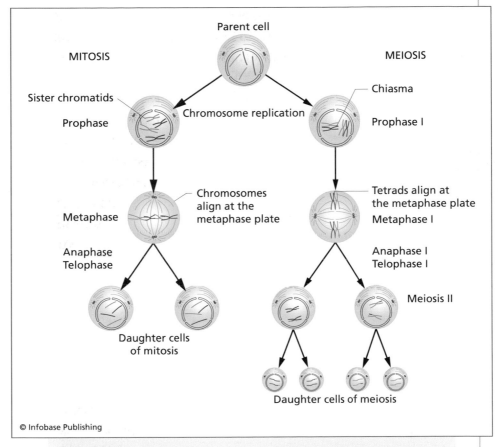

Parent cell

MITOSIS

MEIOSIS

Sister chromatids

Chiasma

Prophase

Chromosome replication

Prophase I

Metaphase

Chromosomes
align at the
metaphase plate

Tetrads align at
the metaphase plate

Metaphase I

Anaphase
Telophase

Anaphase I
Telophase I

Meiosis II

Daughter cells
of mitosis

Daughter cells of meiosis

© Infobase Publishing

FIGURE 3.1 Mitosis *(left)* results in replication of all chromosomes of a diploid organism and their distribution to daughter cells. Stages of mitosis include prophase, metaphase, anaphase, and telophase. Meiosis *(right)* consists of two divisions, meiosis I and meiosis II, and results in four daughter cells each containing the haploid number of chromosomes.

chromosomes (22 autosomes and either an X or a Y) and are said to be **haploid**. If sexually reproducing organisms did not have a haploid stage at some point in their life cycle, the chromosome number would double with each new generation.

In humans, because the gametes are haploid, a diploid fertilized egg (or **zygote**) is formed each time a sperm and egg fuse. As the zygote develops and divides, its diploid set of chromosomes is passed on to newly formed somatic cells by a process of cell division called **mitosis**. Because the chromosomes are replicated once, and the cell divides once, mitosis produces two daughter cells that are genetically identical to the parent cell and to each other (Figure 3.1). A process called **meiosis** produces gametes: A specialized diploid cell goes through one round of chromosome replication and two rounds of cell division. The chromosome

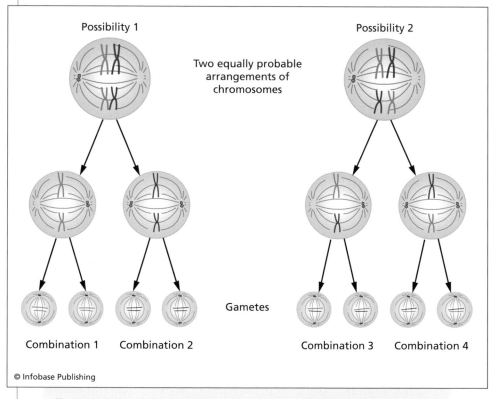

Possibility 1

Two equally probable arrangements of chromosomes

Possibility 2

Gametes

Combination 1   Combination 2   Combination 3   Combination 4

© Infobase Publishing

FIGURE 3.2 Genetic variation results from the independent assortment of chromosomes during meiosis. In the simplified example above, a cell with two pairs of chromosomes results in four possible combinations of paternal and maternal chromosomes in each gamete (sperm or ovum). In humans, because the haploid number is 23, there are 2^{23} (8 million) possible combinations.

number is therefore halved, and the sperm or egg gets a haploid set of 23 different chromosomes, one from each homologous pair (Figure 3.1). Meiosis helps to keep the chromosome number constant from generation to generation (remember that the diploid state is restored when the two haploid sets of chromosomes from the sperm and egg are combined at fertilization); it also increases genetic variation through the variety of combinations of maternal and paternal chromosomes and genes that can be made when the gametes are formed (Figure 3.2).

MENDEL'S LAWS AND GENETICS

Much of the field of genetics is based on the work of Gregor Mendel (1822–1884), an Austrian monk who did breeding experiments with garden peas. By crossing plants with different characteristics and observing and analyzing the results of these crosses, Mendel was able to develop a simple theory to explain how hereditary characteristics, or traits, are transmitted from generation to generation. Although Mendel announced his discoveries in the mid-1860s, they were fully appreciated only after Sutton and Boveri combined them with the newly described theory of meiosis in the early 1900s and formulated the chromosome theory of inheritance. This theory states that meiosis is the process that causes the pattern of inheritance Mendel had observed (and also that hereditary factors, called genes, are located on chromosomes).

To better understand Mendel's theories as they apply to modern genetics, it is helpful to introduce new terms and review some others we have already defined. As mentioned earlier, pairs of homologous autosomes carry the genes for the same traits. This means that every individual carries two homologous genes for most traits, and these genes may be the same or different. Alternate forms or variations of a particular trait or gene are called alleles (Mendel used the term *determinants*).

The term **locus** (plural, *loci*) designates the location of a particular gene on a chromosome; alleles therefore occupy corresponding loci, or locations, on homologous chromosomes. When the two homologous genes consist of identical alleles, the individual is homozygous for that trait; when the alleles are different, the individual is heterozygous. The physical appearance, or manifestation, of a genetic trait is called its *phenotype*, and the genetic makeup (DNA sequence) producing that trait is called its *genotype*.

Mendel wanted to know how the traits of an individual are passed on from generation to generation. His studies of inheritance used strains of peas that varied in seven traits (pea color and shape, flower color and placement, peapod color and shape, and plant size), each of which could show up in either of two easily distinguished phenotypes. Mendel studied three generations of pea plants and always began with **true breeding** plants. True or pure breeding lines of plants are plants that, when self-pollinated (crossed with themselves), always produce offspring with the same phenotype as the parent. Mendel used these true breeders for the parental (or P1) generation and crossed two parental plants with different phenotypes to get the first filial (or F1) generation. He then self-pollinated the F1 plants to get the second filial (or F2) generation. Mendel kept careful records of his crosses and recorded the appearance of each trait in all of the F1 and F2 offspring.

Mendel began by studying one trait at a time, starting with pea shape. Crossing a parental line that always produced round peas with one that always gave wrinkled peas, he observed that every F1 hybrid plant from this crossing had round peas (Figure 3.3). When these F1 **monohybrids** were crossed with themselves, Mendel found that, despite all the F1 plants having had round peas, 1,850 of the 7,344 plants in the F2 generation had wrinkled peas. Thus, the wrinkled trait that had disappeared in the F1 reappeared in the F2 generation. Mendel called the wrinkled pea

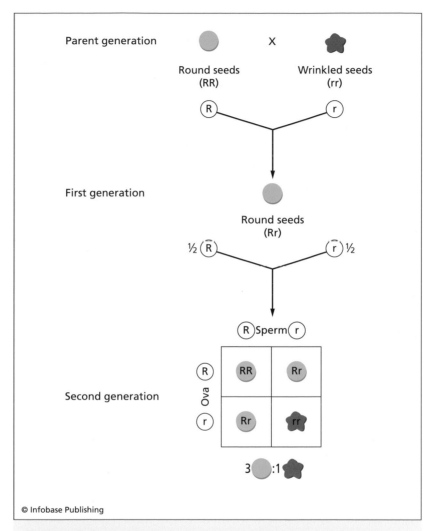

Parent generation

Round seeds (RR)   X   Wrinkled seeds (rr)

R   r

First generation

Round seeds (Rr)

½ R   r ½

R Sperm r

Second generation

Ova

	R	r
R	RR	Rr
r	Rr	rr

3 :1

© Infobase Publishing

FIGURE 3.3 In this illustration of a monohybrid cross, in the parental generation, round seeds (RR) are crossed with wrinkled seeds (rr). In the first generation (F1), all seeds appear to be round (Rr). In the second generation, however, the seeds are in a 3:1 ratio of round to wrinkled. The phenotype ratio is 3:1, but the genotype ratio is 1:2:1.

allele **recessive** because it appeared to recede in the F1 generation; he called the round pea allele **dominant** because it dominated in the F1 generation.

Mendel was the first to use the terms *dominant* and *recessive* to describe how alleles (which he called genetic determinants) interact at the level of the phenotype in heterozygotes. Dominance occurs when the phenotype of one allele (the dominant one) masks that of the other (recessive), so the phenotype of the heterozygote is the same as that of a homozygote for the dominant trait. For the recessive phenotype to show up, the individual must be homozygous (have two copies) for the recessive allele. The term *dominance* is also used today in descriptions of other phenotypic interactions between alleles; these include **incomplete dominance**, which occurs when a heterozygous condition leads to the blending of the two alleles in the phenotype (for example, the F1 generation of a cross between a pure red and a pure white snapdragon is all pink flowers), and **codominance,** which occurs when both alleles show up in the phenotype (for example, the AB blood type discussed in Chapter 1).

A trained mathematician, Mendel easily noticed that the ratio of 5,494 round to 1,850 wrinkled peas that appeared in the F2 generation was about 3:1. After getting ratios of about 3 dominant to 1 recessive phenotype for each of the other 6 traits he examined, Mendel formed a hypothesis. Although the concepts of meiosis, chromosomes, and genes were not yet known, Mendel realized that, to get the results he did, inherited factors (now called genes) had to segregate (separate) from each other as the gametes were formed. Using modern terminology, Mendel's law of **segregation** states that the two alleles of a single homologous gene pair separate from each other when gametes are formed; half the gametes carry one allele, while half carry the other. Thus, homologous genes from maternal and paternal chromosomes are separated from each other when they are distributed to the gametes during meiosis. Mendel realized that two factors must be involved in producing each physical trait in the offspring and that only one factor for each trait gets passed on from each parent.

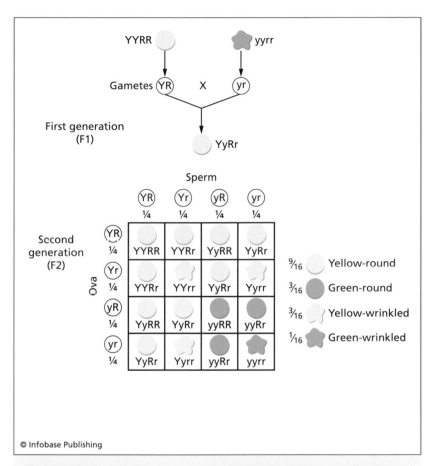

FIGURE 3.4 This illustration of a dihybrid cross demonstrates the Law of Independent Assortment. In the parental generation, yellow-round seeds (YYRR) are crossed with green-wrinkled seeds (yyrr). In the first generation (F1), all seeds appear to be yellow and round (YyRr). In the second generation (F2), the seeds are in a phenotypic ratio of 9:3:3:1, but in a genotype ratio of 1:1:2:2:4:2:2:1:1.

Mendel next analyzed crosses involving alleles of two different genes. For the P1 generation, Mendel used plants that were true breeders for either the two dominant or the two recessive alleles of both traits. Mendel found that, although all of the F1 generation **dihybrids** possessed the dominant phenotype for both traits, the F2 generation had a 9:3:3:1 ratio of phenotypes

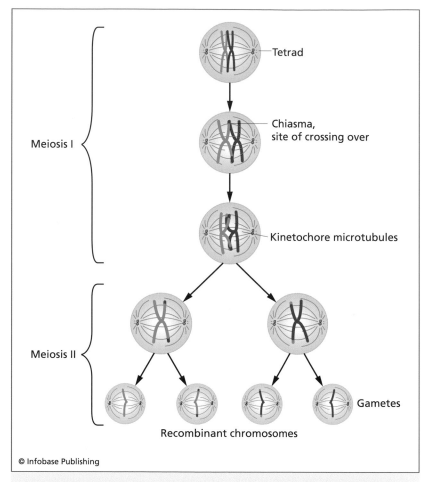

Tetrad

Chiasma, site of crossing over

Meiosis I

Kinetochore microtubules

Meiosis II

Gametes

Recombinant chromosomes

© Infobase Publishing

FIGURE 3.5   This illustration of crossing over between aligned regions of homologous chromosomes during the early phase (prophase) of meiosis results in recombination of genetic information and thereby variation in gametes. On average, there are two to three crossovers per chromosome pair.

made up various combinations of recessive and dominant traits for the two different loci (Figure 3.4). Looking at ratios for each of the two traits individually, Mendel saw that each was present in a 3:1 ratio. He realized that the genes for the two traits had to have been inherited independently of each other.

This phenomenon became known as Mendel's law of **independent assortment**, a theory that explains how a gamete can get a mixture of maternal and paternal genes for different traits. Thus, genes for different traits behave independently of one another in meiosis because alleles on nonhomologous chromosomes are randomly distributed to the gametes. In a dihybrid cross, individuals have two different alleles at two loci, which are on nonhomologous chromosomes, and these are randomly distributed to the gametes.

Mendelian genetics applies to humans as well as pea plants. Mendel's laws were worked out by doing many pea plant crosses and counting many thousands of offspring, something that is not possible with humans. The inheritance of genetic traits in humans can, however, be analyzed by *pedigrees* or family trees that show the occurrence of phenotypes (and alleles) in many generations of related people.

SOURCES OF GENETIC VARIABILITY IN NUCLEAR DNA

One of the main reasons DNA profiling works so well in convicting the guilty and exonerating the innocent is that (with the exception of identical twins) no two individuals have the same overall DNA sequence in their chromosomes. This variability in genetic material is a result of various mechanisms that have been working together over many generations. Two of these mechanisms occur during meiosis. As stated before, the *independent assortment* of genes on different chromosomes leads to different combinations of maternal and paternal chromosomes in the gametes. In addition, even two different maternal and paternal genes located on the same chromosome (*linked genes*) can recombine, if these genes are far apart. This process, called **crossing over**, involves a physical exchange of segments of DNA (genes) between homologous chromosomes during the first cell division of meiosis (Figure 3.5). Genetic variability is also produced after

The Innocence Project

DNA is a tool that not only helps convict the guilty but also helps exonerate the innocent. The Innocence Project, founded by Barry Scheck and Peter Neufeld in 1992, has as its mission the use of postconviction DNA testing to exonerate those who have been wrongfully convicted. As of October 2006, 183 people have been exonerated and are now free to conduct their lives as they wish. Many of these people have already served lengthy prison terms. For example, Orlando Bosquete served 23 years after being convicted because of an eyewitness misidentification. He was exonerated from the crimes of burglary and sexual assault in 2006. Some exonerees even faced capital punishment. A case in point is that of Larry Peterson. At his trial in 1989, the state's key witness and two other men claimed in their testimony that Peterson confessed to them that he had raped and murdered the victim. A state expert using microscopy was able to match six pubic hairs and a head hair fragment from the victim's body and crime scene to Peterson. In addition, four witnesses claimed that they saw fresh fingernail scratches on Peterson's arms in the days following the murder. DNA testing ultimately showed that spermatozoa from the victim's mouth and blood underneath the victim's fingernail did not belong to Larry Peterson, but came from some other male. Furthermore, the six "matching" hairs were actually those of the victim, not Peterson. The state's witness subsequently admitted that he had lied about Peterson making a confession.

gamete formation. This is because mating and fertilization are random processes; any of the different haploid sperms and eggs formed by meiosis can be combined in the zygote.

A major source of genetic variability that does not involve **recombination** between maternal and paternal DNA is mutation, which is a change in one or more of the nucleotide bases in the DNA. If mutations occur in the DNA of a cell that produces gametes, these DNA changes will be passed on from generation to generation. Most of the genetic variability found today initially arose through such mutations.

TYPES OF GENETIC VARIABILITY USED FOR FORENSIC DNA ANALYSIS

There are a number of features of genes and chromosomes that allow forensic scientists to differentiate the DNA of two individuals. These types of genetic variability include those found in short tandem repeats, Y chromosomes, and mitochondrial DNA.

Short Tandem Repeats (STRs)

A short tandem repeat (STR) is a DNA locus containing short segments of DNA (usually four nucleotides long for forensic DNA analysis) that are repeated one after another (in tandem) in differing numbers throughout the population. STR DNA segments do not code for proteins or other phenotype characteristics, and therefore no dominance exists for these loci. Both the maternal and paternal alleles for each homologous STR locus are present in an individual; a person is heterozygous for a particular STR if the maternal and paternal alleles differ; a person is homozygous for that locus if the alleles are identical. The detectable differences in STR alleles are caused by size variations created by differences in the number of times the four-base units are repeated.

The STRs that are used for forensic DNA analysis are all highly *polymorphic*, which means they are present in many forms in the population. The different STRs chosen for DNA identification all assort independently of each other because they are either located on different chromosomes or are far apart on the same chromosome. Thus, the **probability** of a person having any particular STR allele can be multiplied by the probability of them having any other, leading to the great **power of discrimination** achieved when many different STRs are examined together (see the discussion on **product rule** in Chapter 8).

Y Chromosome Inheritance: Paternal Inheritance

As mentioned previously, the sex chromosomes are represented differently in the sexes; males have an X and a Y chromosome and females have two X chromosomes. The X and Y chromosomes differ from each other in their physical structure and in many of the genes that they carry. A **sex-linked** gene is one that is located on the X or the Y chromosome. While homologous autosomes carry genes for the same traits, only small parts of the X and Y sex chromosomes have the same genes. If a sex-linked gene is carried only on the X chromosome, a female will have two copies, whereas a male will have only one copy; genes that are linked to the Y chromosome will have only one copy in a male and no copies in a female.

Y chromosome-linked genes are now being used for forensic DNA analysis. Since the Y chromosome is passed directly from father to son, the analysis of STRs or other genetic markers on the Y chromosome is useful for tracing relationships among males. Because females lack the region of DNA examined in Y-STR analysis, only male DNA will produce results for these loci. Y-STR analysis is therefore very useful in sexual assault cases in which DNA from the male perpetrator is frequently mixed with

World Trade Center

On September 11, 2001, two commercial aircraft crashed into the two towers of the World Trade Center, killing nearly 3,000 men, women, and children. The mass murder was committed by operatives of Al Qaeda masterminded by Osama Bin Laden. The crime scene and all of those within it experienced extraordinary thermal and physical trauma as the mighty towers collapsed into two heaps of rubble. Many bodies were ground into small fragments, while others were completely cremated. Family members of the deceased asked for proof that their loved ones had been lost in the attack. It became vital to reliably identify the bodies and body parts by comparing recovered DNA to the DNA of exemplars in the form of toothbrushes, combs, and hairbrushes, or to the DNA of close relatives. While most of the identifications were obtained through DNA analysis, other methods of identification proved very useful as well. For example, dental records were compared to victims' teeth.

In many instances, recovered DNA was badly degraded making it impossible to rely upon standard DNA analysis testing. The Office of Chief Medical Examiner's DNA laboratory, under the leadership of Dr. Robert Shaler, developed new methods and modified existing procedures to obtain identifying information from human remains. Relatively few samples provided the laboratory with complete, 13 locus, genetic profiles. In addition, mitochondrial DNA analysis was used to type the highly degraded crime scene specimens since this typing method works best under these conditions. Although the majority of mitochondrial DNA profiles

(continues)

(continued from page 31)

are unique, many of these profiles have not been definitive in identifying victims. The remainder of the unidentified specimens have been preserved in the hope that future
improvements in DNA technology will provide absolute
identification of the World Trade Center victims.

the female victim's DNA, a situation that might mask the male
DNA in standard STR testing.

As stated earlier, the markers chosen for standard forensic
STR DNA profiling are **diploid** and assort independently of each
other. Because of this, their probabilities can be multiplied when
more than one of these STRs are examined. The genes used for
Y-STR analysis are clustered on the Y chromosome, with no
complement on the maternal X; they are therefore haploid and
inherited as a unit from father to son. This means they are not
subject to the product rule in frequency determination and,
thus, Y-STR analysis does not have the discrimination power
of standard STR analysis. A more detailed description of how Y
chromosome STRs are used for human identification in forensic
analysis is presented in Chapter 7.

Mitochondrial DNA (mtDNA): Maternal Inheritance

As indicated in Chapter 2, not all of the DNA in a cell is located
within the nucleus. The mitochondria (singular, mitochondrion) are cytoplasmic structures (organelles) involved in
energy production. Although mitochondria contain their own

DNA **genomes**, mitochondrial genes are inherited in a different manner from nuclear genes because the zygote's mitochondria come only from the mother's egg. (The father's sperm contributes only nuclear DNA to the new embryo.) For this reason, all sons and daughters have the same **mitochondrial DNA (mtDNA)** as their mothers, and mtDNA is passed on, virtually unchanged, from one generation to the next through the maternal line of a family. No meiosis is involved in mtDNA replication, and therefore no segregation of alleles or independent assortment takes place. Since little to no genetic recombination occurs on the mitochondrial chromosome, all genes are inherited as if they were a single unit. Because only maternal DNA is present, mtDNA can be considered haploid for mitochondrial genes. In addition, mtDNA contains no STRs and is analyzed, instead, for the sequence of bases in its DNA. (The mitochondrial genome is described in Chapters 2 and 6.)

Like Y-STR analysis, mtDNA analysis is not as definitive as ordinary STR analysis. MtDNA analysis is typically used when samples cannot be analyzed by other methods. Older biological samples that do not contain cellular material with nuclei (such as, hair, bones, and teeth) cannot be analyzed for STRs, but can be analyzed for mtDNA. Thus, mtDNA analysis has become extremely valuable in the investigation of old cases that have gone unsolved for many years. In addition, it can be an important technique in missing person investigations in which the mtDNA profile of unidentified remains can be compared with that of a possible maternal relative. For a more complete discussion of forensic mtDNA analysis, see Chapter 6.

4

Procedures in Forensic DNA Analysis

Most biological materials that are left at a crime scene contain nuclear DNA and can be used for forensic DNA analysis. For a DNA profile to be accepted in a court of law, however, the evidence must be shown to have been collected carefully with an established chain of custody. The chain of custody documents who was in control of the evidence at any time, from the moment that it was collected to the time that it is introduced into evidence in the courtroom. To provide the material necessary for comparison to the crime scene evidence, DNA samples are also collected from suspects and individuals whose DNA may have been left at the scene merely because they lived, worked, or visited there (elimination specimens). These samples are usually taken in the form of blood or cells swabbed from the inner cheek.

In the laboratory, the cells are separated from the substrate (swab or fabric) by agitation in a minimal amount of liquid. The first step needed for any kind of DNA testing is to isolate the DNA and separate it from the other cell components, a procedure known as DNA **extraction**. The particular extraction method used may depend on the type of evidence that is collected, the amount of DNA it contains, and the methods by which it will be analyzed.

Common extraction methods for forensic DNA analysis use **Chelex 100** beads, solid-phase commercial kits, or organic extraction. Forensic DNA laboratories most frequently use the Chelex method, which is less expensive and faster than other methods. With all extraction methods, care must be taken to avoid contamination between the samples as well as contamination by extraneous DNA. In Chelex extraction, the cellular material is boiled with Chelex beads, a procedure that breaks cells open and releases the DNA. Chelex (an ion-exchange resin suspension) protects the DNA by binding to magnesium ions, which enzymes that destroy DNA need to function. After boiling, the sample is centrifuged. The Chelex and all cellular components except the DNA form a tight pellet at the bottom of the tube. The solution above the pellet, which contains the extracted DNA, is then transferred to a new tube. Extracted DNA is usually stored frozen at -20°C or -80°C until it is used. The boiling that is necessary for Chelex extraction causes the DNA strands to separate, but this is not a problem. The currently employed methods of DNA analysis (discussed later) use separated DNA strands.

Since most DNA analysis methods work well only within a particular range of DNA concentrations, it is usually necessary to know how much human DNA is present in an extracted sample before the DNA is analyzed. Most of the methods that are used to determine DNA concentration (for example, **slot blot devices** used with **probes** specific for human DNA, and real-time, quantitative PCR) compare the results for the test sample of extracted DNA with the results for calibrated standards that contain known quantities of DNA. The concentration of the extracted sample is determined by seeing which of the known DNA concentration standards it matches (Figure 4.1).

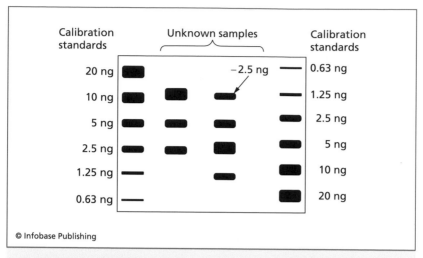

© Infobase Publishing

FIGURE 4.1 DNA is quantified using a device known as a slot blot. The quantity of DNA in each unknown sample is determined by visually comparing the sample band intensity with those of a serial dilution of a known standard DNA ranging from 20 to 0.63 nanograms (ng).

RESTRICTION FRAGMENT LENGTH POLYMORPHISM

The first DNA analysis method that was used in court for DNA identification was restriction fragment length polymorphism (RFLP). In RFLP, large pieces of double-stranded DNA are chopped up by restriction enzymes, which cut the DNA at specific sequences of bases known as restriction endonuclease recognition sites. This technique differentiates people from each other by the pattern that their DNA segments make when they are separated by size. The presence or absence of particular recognition sites in a DNA sample produces different lengths of DNA fragments. These fragments are then separated by gel **electrophoresis** (see page 40) and detected by **hybridization** with DNA probes that bind to complementary DNA sequences in the sample. RFLP is no longer used for forensic human DNA identification and has been replaced by methods that use the polymerase chain reaction (PCR). Because PCR-based methods increase the number of copies of a relatively small segment of DNA, less crime scene DNA is necessary, and this DNA can be analyzed even if it is somewhat **degraded**; RFLP, on the other hand, requires relatively large amounts of undegraded DNA.

POLYMERASE CHAIN REACTION

The PCR method produces millions or billions of exact copies of a particular sequence of DNA, a process called DNA **amplification**, and is sometimes referred to as molecular Xeroxing. DNA amplification by PCR allows biological samples containing much less DNA than is necessary for RFLP to be analyzed for DNA identification.

PCR involves the use of **primers**, which are laboratory-prepared short segments of DNA (18–30 nucleotides long) that specify which region of the DNA will be copied. Two different primers (a forward and a reverse primer) are used for each particular sequence to be amplified, and each primer attaches to a complementary region on one of the separated DNA strands (at either end of the DNA segment to be copied). By constructing PCR primers with the appropriate nucleotide sequences, any particular segment of DNA may be amplified.

A sample that is to undergo PCR must contain the following reagents: the DNA to be amplified (called the **template DNA**), a special type of DNA **polymerase** (for example, Taq polymerase, which comes from bacteria that live in hot springs and functions well at high temperatures), the four building blocks of DNA in a **deoxyribonucleotide triphosphate (dNTP)** form (for example, dATP, dTTP, dGTP, and dCTP), as well as a buffer solution and salts necessary for the DNA polymerase to function (such as, $MgCl_2$). The PCR process mimics the steps used when DNA replicates in a cell, but PCR uses temperature changes to accomplish these steps.

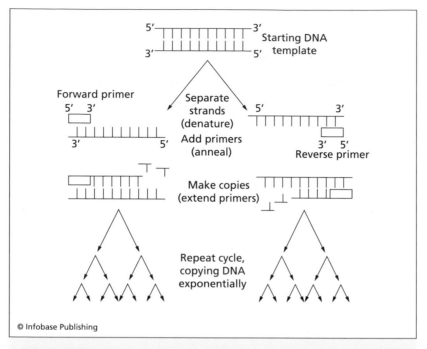

5'━━━━━━━3'
3'━━━━━━━5' Starting DNA template

Forward primer
5' 3'

Separate strands (denature)

5' ━━━━━━━ 3'

3' 5'
Reverse primer

Add primers (anneal)

Make copies (extend primers)

Repeat cycle, copying DNA exponentially

© Infobase Publishing

FIGURE 4.2 The polymerase chain reaction amplifies the quantity of template DNA in the sample. Heating causes the strands of the template DNA to separate; cooling allows the primers to bind to single stranded template DNA; raising the temperature allows new complementary DNA to be formed by extension from the primers. Each cycle of the reaction results in a doubling of the target DNA. After 30 cycles, billions of copies of the region of interest are replicated.

A PCR cycle has three basic steps (Figure 4.2). In the first step (denaturation), the DNA is heated to about 94°C to separate the double-stranded DNA segment, or sequence, into two strands. In the next step (annealing), the temperature is lowered (usually to about 60°C) so that the (single-stranded) primers can bind to each of the single-stranded segments of the target DNA regions by **complementary base pairing**. In the third step (extension), the temperature is raised somewhat (usually to about 72°C) to a temperature at which the enzyme DNA polymerase can add the appropriate nucleotide bases (again by complementary base pairing), and thereby replicate the DNA. The three-step cycle is usually repeated 28 to 30 times. With each completed cycle, the amount of DNA is doubled, and the total amount of DNA continues to grow exponentially as PCR progresses.

PCR OF SHORT TANDEM REPEATS

Short tandem repeat (STR) technology is the method used most frequently for forensic casework. An STR is a DNA locus that contains short segments (usually four bases long) of DNA that are repeated one after another. The human population has a great deal of variability in the length of the repeated regions in the different STRs. This variability, created by differences in the number of times that the units of four bases are repeated, is used to distinguish one DNA profile from another.

Each individual has two alleles (one maternal and one paternal) for each STR locus. The analysis of these autosomal STRs produces the profiles that are used in courts for DNA identification. The Y chromosome (present only in males) also contains STRs. Y-STRs are present in only one copy in each male individual, and therefore cannot discriminate autosomal STRs. They are, however, frequently used to help distinguish DNA profiles in samples containing mixtures of DNA from multiple individuals.

The primers used for PCR of STRs are complementary to the regions of the STR locus that lay outside (flank) the area of tandem repeats. In the currently used methods of forensic DNA analysis, one of the two primers (the forward primer) is labeled with a fluorescent dye (**fluorochrome**). The different alleles of the various STR loci must be distinguished by color as well as by size when many STR loci are amplified together (see **multiplex** PCR section); so, different fluorochromes are used to label loci that overlap in size. The dyes most commonly used to label STR primers are FAM (blue), JOE (green), ROX (red), and TAMRA or NED (yellow). Commercial kits containing appropriate fluorochrome-labeled primers are available for autosomal STR and Y-STR analysis.

ELECTROPHORESIS AND DETECTION OF STRS

Because DNA has a negative charge in solution, it always moves from the negative electrode (**cathode**) to the positive electrode (**anode**) when subjected to an electrical field (electrophoresis). DNA analysis uses two types of electrophoresis: gel and capillary electrophoresis (CE).

Gel electrophoresis (GE) was the DNA separation method used for RFLP analysis, and for STR analysis before appropriate CE instruments became available. The use of CE results in a more rapid and less labor intensive analysis. GE is still used to verify that amplification of template DNA was successful and to separate amplified fragments of DNA based on their size. The gel in GE is made from agarose or polyacrylamide and is covered with a buffer solution. Depressions (wells) made in the top portion of the gel (close to the negative electrode) are filled with the DNA sample. The current is then turned on, causing the DNA to move out of the well and toward the positive electrode. Because shorter pieces of DNA move through the gel faster than longer pieces, this process separates the DNA fragments by size. DNA fragments of the same size stay together and form "bands" in the gel. A ladder of DNA-fragment-sizing standards (and/or an **allelic ladder**, see next section) is run in some of the gel wells to estimate the length of the various bands. It does this by matching the distance the DNA traveled in a particular band to the ladder standard(s) that traveled a similar distance. With GE, bands are detected following electrophoresis by hybridizing to labeled probes (RFLP), staining the DNA with silver (old STR method), or using detectable fluorochrome-labeled primers in the PCR reaction (STR).

STR analysis is usually done using capillary electrophoresis instruments for the separation, detection, and analysis of STR fragments of different sizes. Most of the CE instruments used for this purpose in the United States are Prism® Genetic Analyzers (models 310 and 3100) made by Applied Biosystems Inc., although other companies are now manufacturing and selling instruments capable of capillary electrophoresis and sequencing.

Capillary electrophoresis uses a long, narrow glass tube or capillary containing a special polymer solution that permits DNA fragments to be separated by size. (Instruments containing many capillaries operating at once have been developed for use in laboratories with high-volume workloads.) The PCR-amplified STRs are added to the capillary, and during elec-

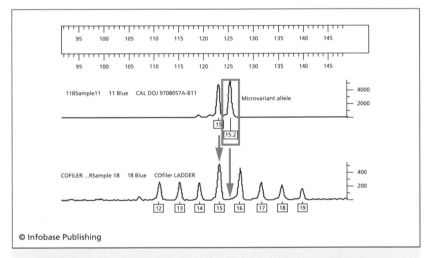

FIGURE 4.3 This illustration shows how software is designed to identify an allele by comparing its position (length in base pairs) to an allelic ladder.

trophoresis the polymer within the tube allows the smaller fragments to move faster than the larger ones. In the separation process, the fragments are exposed to a laser beam, which permits the different fluorescent dyes attached to the primers to emit light of particular wavelengths. The instrument detects the wavelengths emitted. This allows the comparison of the movement (measured as migration time) of test sample fragments with standard ladder fragments of known sizes, as well as with those of an allelic ladder made up of most of the known fragment sizes (alleles) for a particular STR locus. A series of peaks (called an electropherogram) is produced, showing the relative **fluorescence** of each STR fragment labeled with a particular dye versus its migration time. The instrument's computer software processes the information and gives the size of the different alleles in the electropherogram and their genotype (the number of repeats they contain) relative to the standards. Alleles that fall between two allelic ladder standards contain an incomplete repeat (fewer than four bases) and are called **microvariants** (Figure 4.3).

At least 13 STR loci are required for a DNA profile to be uploaded into the Combined DNA Index System (**CODIS**), operated by the Federal Bureau of Investigation (FBI). To conserve the evidence sample and decrease the time and effort expended for DNA analysis, many STR loci are amplified in the same PCR reaction (multiplex PCR) and run together in the same capillary. To be distinguishable by CE, the DNA fragments must have different migration times because of their different sizes. Since many of the alleles of the 13 CODIS STR loci overlap in size, primers for these overlapping loci are tagged with different dyes to distinguish them by color and size. Commercial manufacturers have developed multiplex PCR kits that can amplify 16 loci at once, with all alleles and loci distinguishable from each other.

MITOCHONDRIAL DNA ANALYSIS AND CE SEQUENCING

STR DNA typing does not work for all biological samples. MtDNA analysis can, however, frequently be used to obtain some DNA typing information when samples contain DNA that is highly degraded or insufficient for nuclear DNA STR analysis. Older biological samples that contain very little nucleated cellular material (for example, hair, bones, and teeth) cannot be analyzed for STRs, but such samples can frequently be analyzed for mtDNA. Although nuclear DNA contains much more infor-

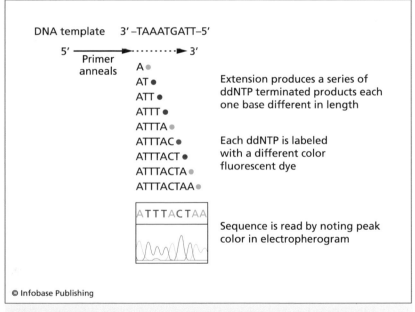

FIGURE 4.4 DNA sequencing uses fluorescently labeled dideoxy terminator nucleotide triphosphates (ddNTPs) together with normal deoxynucleotide triphosphates (dNTPs). The ddATP, ddGTP, ddCTP, and ddTTP molecules are each labeled with a different fluorescent dye. The procedure uses primers and a DNA polymerase. Any growing chain of DNA will cease to extend if it incorporates a ddNTP rather than a dNTP. A DNA sequencer can determine the length of extension products, each of which can be distinguished by its fluorescence (color) emission.

mation than mtDNA, it is present in only two copies per cell; a cell contains hundreds to thousands of copies of mtDNA.

The mitochondrial genome and its pattern of inheritance were described in Chapters 2 and 3. For forensic purposes, mtDNA is considered to be inherited solely from one's mother. Because a mother passes her mtDNA to all of her children, all siblings and maternal relatives have the same mtDNA sequence, and unlike nuclear DNA, mtDNA is not unique to an individual. Although this pattern of maternal inheritance is frequently helpful in missing persons or mass disaster investigations, it reduces the significance of a match in forensic cases.

MtDNA is analyzed by sequencing, a process that determines the order (sequence) of the DNA nucleotides in a DNA segment. The particular regions of the mtDNA genome sequenced are those that are the most variable among individuals, that is, the hypervariable control regions HV1 and HV2 described in Chapter 2. Methods for sequencing DNA are usually performed with the same CE instruments that are used for STR analysis; different PCR and CE analysis strategies, however, are used for this type of DNA analysis.

For mtDNA sequencing, the DNA of each **hypervariable region** is first amplified. The amplified PCR product for each particular region is then individually used in another PCR reaction, in which, in addition to the usual dNTP building blocks, special types of nucleotides that stop DNA replication (**dideoxyribonucleotide triphosphates: ddNTPs**) are also present. Each of the four ddNTPs is labeled with a fluorescent dye of a different color. When a ddNTP is added to a growing segment of DNA instead of a dNTP, DNA extension stops immediately, and no new nucleotides are added. Because both types of NTPs are present, different PCR products will be terminated at different points on the DNA template, and a mixture containing a series of DNA fragments, each differing by one base pair in length, is formed (Figure 4.4).

CE then separates these fragments, and because each has the label of the last base (ddNTP) added, the entire sequence of bases in the DNA region examined can be obtained. After the sequence is generated, it is compared to a reference sequence for mtDNA, and differences are noted. MtDNA coming from the same person or from a person with the same maternal lineage is expected to have the same DNA sequence and therefore the same differences from the reference sequence. The interpretation of mtDNA sequence data is discussed in Chapter 6.

5 Interpretation of Autosomal STR DNA Analysis

Analysis of STR loci and mtDNA sequencing techniques for human identification are the most important tests used in crime labs today. STR methods include genotyping of the autosomal (nonsex chromosome) and Y chromosome STR loci. Mitochondrial DNA analysis is more labor intensive and less informative than nuclear STR techniques, but it can be very useful in providing information that we could not obtain otherwise. Interpretation of mitochondrial and Y-chromosome STR DNA test results will be covered more completely in Chapters 6 and 7, respectively. This chapter deals with the interpretation of autosomal STR typing results and the CODIS database.

A number of multiplex STR test kits are available for human identification. Multiplexing allows the analyst to amplify and genotype a number of genetic loci simultaneously, thereby conserving evidence and providing a great deal of information about the source of the sample under study. Many laboratories use a combination of two commercial kits known as AmpF*l*STR **Cofiler**™ and AmpF*l*STR **Profiler Plus**™; others use a single multiplex kit known as AmpF*l*STR Identifiler™ to achieve the same goal. The former test kits include the reagents to analyze 13

STR loci plus **amelogenin**. The latter kit allows for the analysis of 15 STR loci plus amelogenin. All three kits are manufactured by Applied Biosystems Inc. (ABI). Other forensic DNA testing laboratories use multiplex kits manufactured by Promega Corp., including the GenePrint PowerPlex® 1.1 (8 loci), GenePrint PowerPlex® 2.1 (9 loci), and the PowerPlex®16 System. Regardless of which test kits a laboratory uses, it is important that all 13 CODIS loci be included in the testing.

CODIS DATABASE

CODIS refers to the Combined DNA Indexing System database that the FBI established as a pilot project in 1990. In 1994, Congress passed the DNA Identification Act, which formalized the authority of the FBI to establish this national database. CODIS consists of a national database (NDIS), state databases (SDIS), and local databases (LDIS). The NDIS became operational in 1998. It contains profiles that have been uploaded from various state DNA testing laboratories through their respective SDIS systems. Laboratories desiring to enter data into (or to search data already held in) the CODIS database must meet appropriate standards to ensure reliability of their test results.

There are several CODIS databases, each dealing with a different form of DNA analysis. The autosomal STR database includes the following 13 loci: D3S1358, D16S539, THO1, TPOX, CSF1PO, D7S820, VWA, FGA, D8S1179, D21S11, D18S51, D5S818, and D13S317. CODIS databases include a **convicted offender database** and an **evidentiary database** as well as specialized databases dealing with missing persons. Individuals who commit certain criminal acts described as **felonies**, are required to submit a DNA specimen and their genetic profiles are included in the convicted offender database. DNA obtained from crime scene evidence is included in the evidentiary (crime scene) database. National databases are extremely important for law enforcement involving crimes committed by repeat offenders. They also help in cases of crimes committed by the same individual in different jurisdictions (states, counties). Requirements for submission of a DNA specimen vary from state to state. Some states now include or will soon include all individuals arrested for any serious criminal activity (**misdemeanors** and felonies).

What follows is a description of Cofiler and Profiler test kit analysis and how results are interpreted. The AmpF*l*STR Cofiler™ multiplex test kit allows for the amplification and genotyping of six STR loci (D3S1358, D16S539, THO1, TPOX, CSF1PO, D7S820) and the locus known as amelogenin, which provides information about the gender of the individual from whom the sample originated. The AmpF*l*STR ProfilerPlus™ test kit allows for the amplification of nine STR loci (D3S1358, VWA, FGA, D8S1179, D21S11, D18S51, D5S818, D13S317, and D7S820) plus amelogenin. Both kits analyze the D3S1358 and D7S820 loci, so when both kits are used to type a single sample, genotyping will provide information for 13 STR loci and amelogenin.

Following PCR amplification of DNA, the samples are injected into a capillary electrophoresis system or placed into wells in a gel electrophoresis system. As explained previously, the fragments of DNA are separated based on their size. Amplified DNA products are also separated based on color. To allow testing of multiple loci, amplified DNA fragments are labeled with dyes that fluoresce specific colors when excited by certain wavelengths of light. In this way, alleles of different loci with similar sizes can still be differentiated based on which color of light they emit. Peaks from amplified DNA products are measured in terms of **relative fluorescence units (RFUs)**.

Like any other experimental procedure, DNA testing of biological evidence must include positive and negative controls. If these controls do not produce expected results, test results for the questioned samples cannot be trusted and must be repeated. Negative controls include a DNA extraction control and an amplification control. These controls are important to determine if contamination is present in the test results. The extraction control is performed by carrying out the extraction in a tube containing no sample, which is then subjected to PCR; the amplification **control sample**, on the other hand, contains no added template DNA; it checks for contamination introduced during the amplification stage. If there is no contamination, the results for these control samples should be negative.

A **substrate control** is also included in the analysis. The substrate control is a specimen obtained adjacent to a stain of interest. For example, if a bloodstain is found on an item of clothing, an evidence sample is obtained from the bloodstained fabric, and the substrate control sample is taken from an area of the fabric near the stain. Including a substrate control ensures that the DNA found in the stain is not present on or within the underlying fabric.

If the extraction control or the amplification control produces a peak higher than 100 RFU, then the results for all the samples run with this control must be considered **inconclusive** and they must be retested. If a peak or peaks appear on a substrate control, however, the control results must be interpreted, and the results for the other samples can be considered conclusive. A substrate control is not a negative control and may contain DNA relevant to a case. A positive control is also included every time a test is done and must produce the appropriate alleles to indicate that the test is being performed correctly. If the alleles produced by the positive control test differ from the expected alleles, the test must be considered inconclusive and all samples must be retested.

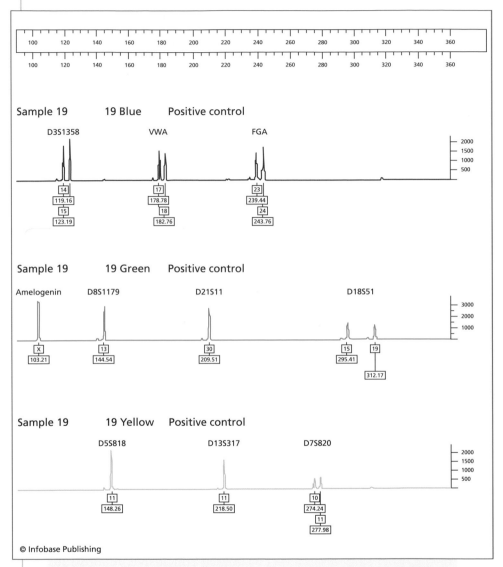

FIGURE 5.1 Typing results for the positive control DNA provided in the AmpF*I*STR Profiler Plus™ kit.

The positive control (Figure 5.1) for the AmpF*I*STR Profiler Plus™ kit has the following expected genotypes:

	D3S1358	VWA	FGA	
Blue Dye:	14, 15	17, 18	23, 24	
	Amelogenin	D8S1179	D21S11	D18S51
Green Dye:	X	13	30	15, 19
	D5S818	D13S317	D7S820	
Yellow Dye:	11	11	10, 11	

Multiplex test kits also contain an allelic ladder consisting of DNA fragments that reflect all of the common alleles for each of the loci tested (Figure 5.2). In order for the GeneScan® and GenoTyper® software to identify specific alleles in a questioned sample, the unknown fragments must be compared to alleles identified within the ladder. Fragments identified as having a different size from those alleles within the ladder are considered to be "off-ladder" alleles or "microvariants," which are far less common and statistically more significant for human identification. Both software applications have been upgraded in a product known as GeneMapper® software.

The positive control (Figure 5.3) for the AmpF*l*STR Cofiler™ kit has the following genotypes:

	D3S1358	D16S539		
Blue Dye:	14, 15	11, 12		
	Amelogenin	THO1	TPOX	CSF1PO
Green Dye:	X	8, 9.3	8	10, 12
	D7S820			
Yellow Dye:	10, 11			

Profiler Plus	Color	Allele Range in Ladder
D3S1358	Blue	12 to 19
VWA	Blue	11 to 21
FGA	Blue	18 to 30
Amelogenin	Green	X and Y
D8S1179	Green	8 to 19
D21S11	Green	24.2 to 38
D18S51	Green	9 to 26
D5S818	Yellow	7 to 16
D13S317	Yellow	8 to 15
D7S820	Yellow	6 to 15

Cofiler	Color	Allele Range in Ladder
D3S1358	Blue	12 to 19
D16S539	Blue	5 to 15
Amelogenin	Green	X and Y
THO1	Green	5 to 10
TPOX	Green	6 to 13
CSF1PO	Green	6 to 15
D7S820	Yellow	6 to 15

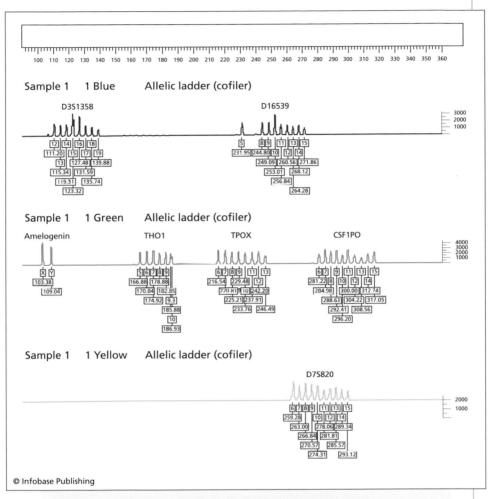

Figure 5.4 Allelic ladder for the AmpF*l*STR Cofiler™ kit.

INTERPRETATION OF MIXTURES OF DNA

Evidence may sometimes consist of a mixture of contributors making the observed pattern more complex. Interpreting mixtures of DNA can sometimes be confusing. Guidelines need to be established and followed for consistent conclusions. These mixtures may consist of biological material from victim(s) and assailant(s), or material from a single individual combined with one or more contaminating sources. If an STR analysis includes even one heterozygous locus with more than two peaks, the sample is most likely a mixture. The overall pattern or genetic profile should, however, be carefully examined before concluding that a mixture exists. One should generally not look at only a single locus to form an opinion. A locus that appears to be a heterozygous genotype (for example, TPOX – 7,12) could be a mixture of two individuals, each of whom is a homozygote at this locus (7,7 and 12,12). In this case, the peak heights may be the same or different, depending on how much of each component is present in the mixture. When examining a single locus, the analyst should consider the possibility that the sample consists of a sole source, a mixture of individuals who are both homozygous (7,7 and 12,12), both heterozygous (7,12 and 7,12), or one homozygous (7,7) and the second heterozygous (7,12).

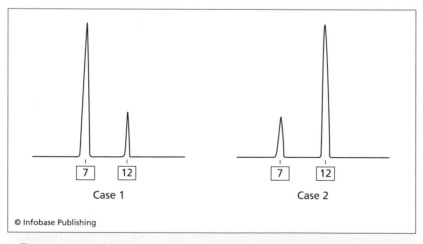

FIGURE 5.5   Mixtures of DNA must be interpreted by analyzing peak heights.

Alternatively, the homozygous genotype could be 12,12, and the heterozygous genotype 7,12. If equal amounts of DNA from each individual are present, then in the first case (7,7 + 7,12) the 7 allele (peak) will have a peak height 3 times as high as the 12, whereas in the second case (7,12 + 12,12) the 12 allele will have a peak height 3 times the height of the 7 peak (Figure 5.5).

The multiplex kits are also designed in such a way that, if all DNA samples are quantified to be within a specific range (approximately 1–5 ng), the resulting peak heights at all loci will be within 25% to 30% of each other (experimentally determined). If alleles are markedly different in peak heights, a mixture of template DNAs should be considered. When DNA samples from two individuals are combined in different quantities, results with variable peak heights require further interpretation.

DEGRADED DNA

DNA degradation refers to the breakdown of relatively large fragments of DNA into smaller fragments. When DNA within evidentiary samples has become degraded, the larger alleles within loci may be decreased in peak height or missing, depending on the amount of DNA breakdown. Thus, the larger allele of a heterozygous genotype may be missing, and the locus can appear as homozygous. In addition, all alleles for the larger STR loci may be missing. This is something that should be considered in samples that are old or have been exposed to environmental factors, such as sunlight, soil, bacteria, or fungi.

When degradation is advanced, the target DNA sequences for the PCR amplification reaction (which must contain both primer annealing sites) also break down. Thus, at any locus (for example, D18S51 with alleles in the range of 274–342 bp), the larger alleles will more likely be lost in a partially degraded sample.

Convicting the Guilty

The science and technology of forensic DNA analysis has dramatically improved over the past 2 decades. Crime laboratories now routinely test for the 13 CODIS loci, Y-STR loci, and mitochondrial DNA. In 1985, when it was recognized that DNA testing could be used to solve crimes of violence, such as murder and rape, DNA was hailed as a revolution in testing for human identification. It has truly been just that.

It is not possible to determine how many criminals are now behind bars because of DNA testing, but the horrific rape and murder of a young woman and her boyfriend is but one example of how DNA testing has been used in forensic science. Mark Barton was ambushed as he was about to leave his San Francisco home for work on July 9, 1999, then taken inside and tied up. His girlfriend of three and a half years was raped as Barton was forced to watch. Barton was shot in the head and killed. His girlfriend was thrown into a closet and shot in the stomach. She survived her injuries, escaped, and called for help. Police retrieved DNA evidence from the home, but unfortunately, due to a severe backlog of cases, the evidence was not tested until 2002. A suspect, Ivory Morton, was arrested in 2003 and convicted of murder. The evidence consisted of a latex glove found at the scene that had traces of Morton's DNA. In addition, ropes found near the glove had Morton's DNA, as well as the DNA of the rape victim and Barton. A current initiative by President George Bush is providing additional funding to clear up the nation's testing backlog. This will help to ensure that evidence is DNA tested earlier, and criminals are taken off the street before committing additional crimes.

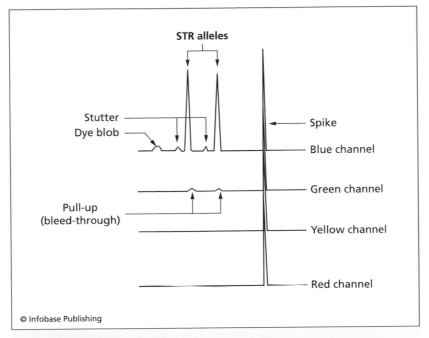

FIGURE 5.6 These amplification artifacts illustrate stutter, pull-up peaks, spikes, and dye blobs.

Partial degradation can be inferred when the AmpF*l*STR Profiler Plus™ Kit is used (to amplify the 9 STR loci and amelogenin). Alleles of the smaller loci D3S1358, D8S1179, and D5S818 are seen, but alleles of the larger loci, D18 and D7, are not seen.

ARTIFACTS IN OBSERVED RESULTS

Sometimes, the results of experimentation can be confusing and difficult to interpret because of the existence of sharp **spikes** or peaks that occur due to electrical noise, incorrect setting of the matrix, and/or unexpected DNA replication problems during PCR (Figure 5.6). The analyst should examine the results carefully to verify that all observed peaks are real, representing specific genes and not a result of an artifact produced during the amplification, fragment separation, or detection processes. Some observed alleles are uncommon and are therefore not included in the allelic ladder. Such alleles, when observed, require authentication. The following are descriptions and explanations of some common artifacts:

- **Stutter:** If examination of the genetic profile indicates a sole contributor, and the printout indicates a small peak, either -4 bp or +4 bp, adjacent to a larger peak. The "-4 bp" stutter is much more common, and the software will sometimes label it as an authentic peak. The "+4 bp" stutter is extremely rare and has to be interpreted carefully, since it may indicate the presence of a mixed specimen. Some loci are more prone to amplify with stutter (for example, VWA) than others. Experimentation shows that, on average, **stutter peak** height ranges from approximately 2 to 14% of the adjacent peak. The software does not report such small −4 bp peaks as alleles.

- **Pull-Up Peaks**: "Pull-ups" of peaks in any color are caused by a very high peak of another color in the same injection. Pull-ups are caused by the inability of the software to remove all overlap, that is, green light components originating from a strong blue signal.

- **Split Peaks:** Sometimes referred to as "N" bands, in which the main allele appears as a split peak. "N" bands are caused by incomplete extra adenine addition (a PCR artifact) and are characterized by a jagged edge on the left side of the peak or a complete split on the top level. The split peak is caused by two fragments differing in size by only a single adenine base.

- **Shoulder Peaks**: Shoulder peaks are approximately 1 to 4 bp smaller or bigger than the main allele. Shoulder peaks are most often apparent on the right side of a large peak, especially if the peak shape appears to have a trailing slope.

- **Spikes in Printout:** Sharp peaks that do not have the characteristics of normally shaped peaks, but rather appear as vertical lines. These spikes may be caused by air bubbles or urea crystals in the capillary. The presence of a spike can sometimes be verified by examining the printout of the calibrator red-size standard for the same injection or any of the other colors. Such "spikes" will occur at the same position for all colors.

- **Noisy or Raised Baseline:** Sometimes the software calls a peak as an allele when that peak is on top of a raised baseline. A raised baseline can be observed when the polymer within the capillary is dirty or there are capillary problems.

- **Dye Artifact or Dye "Blob":** Peak that appears more cup-shaped than a peak. These artifacts (usually blue) appear at a constant position on the printout.

- **Nonspecific Artifacts:** Artifacts that cannot be described by one of the previous categories. Such peaks cannot be reproduced despite repeated testing.

On some rare occasions, a heterozygous genotype may appear as homozygous. This can occur when there is a mutation in the primer-binding site of an allele that prevents one of the primers from annealing as it should. It is also possible for a mutation close to the primer-binding site to block extension of new DNA during amplification. A comparison between evidence and **exemplar** (known) samples based on a locus where both samples were amplified with the same primer sequence is no problem. If the same locus is amplified using different multiplex systems, however, it is possible to obtain a heterozygous type with one multiplex and an apparent homozygote with the second. This occurs because different multiplex kits may use different primers for the same loci, and a mutation may occur in only one of the primer-binding sites. In such a case, the heterozygote type should be considered the correct type. For this reason, all samples from the same case should be tested with the same multiplex system.

Although the interpretation of mixed samples can be difficult, and results from the electrophoresis may include artifacts, careful observation and adherence to the typing protocol will allow accurate conclusions about a sample's genetic profile. The next chapter reviews the interpretation of a mitochondrial DNA sequencing analysis.

Mitochondrial DNA (mtDNA)

6

Chapter 2 provided a description of the structure of the mito-chondrial genome. This chapter focuses more on analysis and interpretation of typing results. When sample size is limited, as is the case when only a small segment of bone, a tooth, or a shaft of hair is found as physical evidence, mitochondrial DNA sequencing is the method of choice to determine the origin of such samples. Mitochondrial DNA sequencing is also useful when an evidentiary biological specimen is degraded by environmental factors or aging, and nuclear DNA testing fails. Mitochondrial DNA is often analyzed in cases when a body is found that has undergone severe decomposition, lost its soft tissues, and become skeletonized. Unlike nuclear DNA, mtDNA is present in high copy number, with hundreds of mitochondria present in most cells.

Mitochondrial DNA is maternally inherited, which means that all first-generation children, male and female, inherit the same mitochondrial genetic profile as their mother. The mtDNA of a man is, however, not usually passed along to his children. Female children, on the other hand, will continue to pass along their mtDNA to their own offspring. In this way, there is a continu-

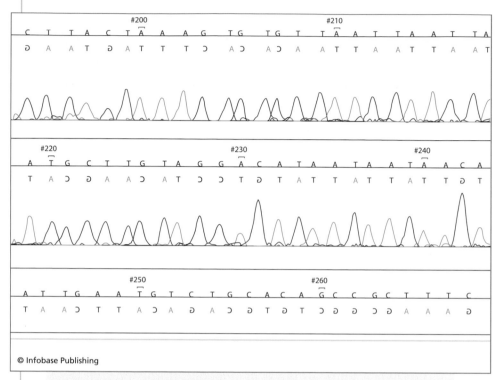

FIGURE 6.1 This small segment of mtDNA that has been sequenced illustrates color peaks representing amplified products terminating in dye labeled A, G, C, and T.

ous line of inheritance of a specific genetic profile from mother to daughter, to granddaughter, and so on. By studying certain mitochondrial DNA sequences, one can determine if a grandchild (male or female) is related to a woman claiming to be the grandmother (Figure 6.1). A woman will also share her mitochondrial DNA profile with her siblings, male and female, and with her maternal relatives, including sisters, aunts, nieces, and cousins. Because the mitochondrial genome does not undergo recombination, the genome is transmitted from generation to generation unchanged in sequence. The only exception to this generality is a mutational event.

The FBI began to examine mitochondrial DNA sequences in biological evidence in June 1996. As described in Chapter 2, the mitochondrial genome is a closed circle of DNA that consists of 16,569 base pairs. The two strands of the molecule are referred to as the heavy (H) and light (L) strands. The former strand has the largest number of guanine nucleotides. These bases have the largest molecular weight of all four DNA building blocks. As a result, the H strand can easily be separated from the L strand by centrifugation. The genome contains regions that code for 36 gene products, including specific proteins and ribonucleic acids that are involved in the structure and function of the mitochondrion as well as a control region, whose purpose is to regulate mitochondrial DNA replication. The control region contains two segments of DNA that are highly polymorphic and described as hypervariable (HV). Thus, the forensic analyst is primarily interested in regions HV1 and HV2. The first, HV1, has a sequence of 342 bp (16,024–16,365) and the second, HV2, has a sequence of 268 bp (73–340). All of these bases (610 bp combined) are sequenced in forensic mtDNA analysis.

It would be very difficult to totally sequence exemplars (known reference samples) and evidentiary items and then report this total sequence information from beginning to end. To avoid any confusion in the comparison of two specimens, the forensic analyst compares each specimen's mtDNA sequence to a reference sequence, and then describes differences found at specific sites. The reference mtDNA, derived primarily from a human placenta, is known as the Anderson sequence. It is also known as the Cambridge reference sequence (CRS) or Oxford sequence. Today, most laboratories use the revised Cambridge sequence (rCRS) as the reference. This revised reference sequence, established in 1999, has corrected a number of sequencing errors in the original 1981 Anderson sequence. Each base in the reference sequence is assigned a number from

1 to 16,569 and forensic analysts use these numbers to compare all other specimens.

Following is a segment of the human mtDNA revised Cambridge reference sequence (light strand):

16021 CTGTTCTTTC ATGGGGAAGC AGATTTGGGT ACCACCCAAG TATTGACTCA CCCATCAACA

16081 ACCGCTATGT ATTTCGTACA TTACTGCCAG CCACCATGAA TATTGTACGG TACCATAAAT

16141 ACTTGACCAC CTGTAGTACA TAAAAACCCA ATCCACATCA AAACCCCCTC CCCATGCTTA

16201 CAAGCAAGTA CAGCAATCAA CCCTCAACTA TCACACATCA ACTGCAACTC CAAAGCCACC

16261 CCTCACCCAC TAGGATACCA ACAAACCTAC CCACCCTTAA CAGTACATAG TACATAAAGC

16321 CATTTACCGT ACATAGCACA TTACAGTCAA ATCCCTTCTC GTCCCCATGG ATGACCCCCC

There are no changes in the HV1 or HV2 in the revised reference sequence. Thus, if the reference sequence is as follows:

GAGCCGGAGC ---------- GCTTGTAGGA
101   110 ---------- 221   230

and an item of evidence is sequenced as

GAGCCGGACC ---------- GGTTGTAGGA
101   110 ---------- 221   230

and the exemplar specimen is sequenced as

GAGCCGGACC ---------- GGTTGTAGGA
101   110 ---------- 221   230

then the differences between each of the two specimens analyzed relative to the reference sequence are recorded in the report as

109C; 222G for the evidence, and 109C; 222G for the suspect.

Thus, the evidence and suspect share the same sequence in the region analyzed. Furthermore, if **deletions** or **additions** are observed in the sequence, these kinds of differences will be noted as well.

The sequencing procedure described in Chapter 4 is performed in both directions, forward and reverse, to verify that the sequence determined is correct. As described earlier, any variation from the reference sequence is noted. In this way, one can compare the variations of the suspect sample with those of the evidence. If they are the same, there is an **inclusion**, meaning a common origin is possible. This result, we say, "cannot exclude the specimens as coming from the same source." If the variations differ, there is an **exclusion,** and no common origin exists.

Mitochondrial DNA and the Scott Peterson Trial

During the Scott Peterson double-homicide trial held in California in 2004, mtDNA analysis of a hair found on a pair of pliers in Peterson's fishing boat was important evidence linking Laci Peterson to that boat. The prosecution expert said that only 1 in 112 Caucasians would be expected to share the same mtDNA profile, and Scott Peterson was excluded as the source of the hair. The prosecutor's theory was that the hair belonged to Laci Peterson. The prosecutor claimed, however, that Laci Peterson had never been on the boat, nor did she know that her husband had bought one. The prosecution believed that she was killed sometime around December 24, 2002; her body was carried onto that boat and thrown overboard into San Francisco Bay. Laci Peterson was pregnant and expecting a boy, to be named Connor. The bodies of Laci and Connor Peterson floated onto the shore and were discovered in 2003 on April 13 (Connor), and April 14 (Laci). Scott Peterson was convicted on November 12, 2004, of first-degree murder of Laci Peterson with special circumstances and second-degree murder of Connor. Peterson is currently on death row at San Quentin Prison in California.

INTERPRETATION OF RESULTS

The FBI has established guidelines for interpreting mitochondrial sequence comparisons. Comparison of known and questioned specimens to the revised Cambridge sequence can result in an exclusion, an inclusion (an inability to exclude), or an inconclusive finding. The Scientific Working Group on DNA Analysis Methods has recommended the following guidelines for analyzing mitochondrial sequence data:

1. If there are two or more differences in the base sequence of the exemplar and evidentiary sequences, one can conclude that there is no common origin between the two specimens. This constitutes an exclusion.

2a. If there is no difference in sequence between the evidentiary and exemplar specimens, then the two specimens may have a common origin, and the analyst should report that a common origin for the two cannot be excluded.

2b. If there is **heteroplasmy** (see page 70) at the same site for both exemplar and evidentiary specimens and identical bases at every other position, you cannot exclude a common origin.

   For example:

   AGCTAGGCA/GCT   [Both A and G are found in the same position
        and   for both specimens]
   AGCTAGGCA/GCT

2c. If there is heteroplasmy in one sample that is not present in the other, but bases at every other position are identical, then you cannot exclude a common origin.

AGCTAGGCA/GCT   [Both A and G are found at a position in one

and   specimen while A or G is found at that site

AGCTAGGC A CT   on the second]

Sometimes, sequencing a segment of DNA results in an ambiguous base at a specific position. We denote this as "N" and designate such sequences as shown follows:

AGCTAGCCNCT and AGCTAGCCACT

or

AGCTAGCCNCT   and AGCNAGCCACT

In either case you still cannot exclude a common origin for the two specimens sequenced.

3.   If there is only one base difference between the exemplar and evidentiary sequences, one must consider this result as **inconclusive.**

STATISTICS

Unlike nuclear STR loci, all sites on the mitochondrial genome are linked, that is, there is only a single mitochondrial chromosome. Therefore, you cannot calculate statistics of the genetic profile using the product rule, as is done for the 13 nuclear STR loci described in Chapter 5. With these nuclear markers, the statistical calculation for the overall genetic profile of a specimen is based on each locus being inherited independently from each of the other 12 loci.

Databases of mitochondrial sequence information have been collected, and it has been shown that 60% of the sequences in a mitochondrial database are unique. Currently, we describe the frequency of a sequence using the **counting method**: if the sequence appears for the first time, and we have thus far examined

6,000 specimens, the frequency of this genetic profile is 1 in 6,001. If the sequence had been found once before in a specimen, then we would indicate a frequency of 2 in 6,001. Statistics based on the database do not accurately reflect the actual frequency of any sequence. The frequency of 1 or 2 in 6,001 clearly understates the rarity of the sequence, primarily because the database is relatively small. We can also express the frequency of a sequence providing 95% confidence limits and the upper and lower limits (the highest frequency estimate and the lowest frequency estimate), to establish a reasonable range of possible values for the profile's actual frequency in the relevant population.

HETEROPLASMY

Heteroplasmy is the existence of more than one mtDNA type in a single individual and at a particular base position in a sequence of bases. There are two kinds of heteroplasmy: length and sequence.

An example of length heteroplasmy is

ATAGACAG**CCCCCCCC**TAG
ATAGACAG**CCCCC**TAG

An example of sequence heteroplasmy

ATAGACAG**A**TACCATG
ATAGACAG**G**TACCATG

Heteroplasmy can exist in both the exemplar (known specimen) and the evidentiary specimen. If the analyst finds heteroplasmy at a specific position in both evidentiary and exemplar specimens, this is helpful in deciding there is an inclusion; a heteroplasmy at a specific position is an important characteristic. Studies have shown that heteroplasmy may differ from tissue to tissue in the same individual, thus, hair and blood may demonstrate different levels and types of heteroplasmy.

Y Chromosome Testing

7

MIXED SAMPLES AND Y CHROMOSOME STRS

PCR amplification of the 13 autosomal (nonsex chromosome) STR loci and the subsequent genotyping analysis has proven to be a highly sensitive and reliable method for identifying individuals who are the sources of biological evidence. At times, however, even this strategy fails to provide the information we seek. For example, testing may not be successful when the amount of sample DNA is insufficient or when the available DNA is severely degraded. In other situations, the analysis is performed successfully but still fails to reveal important information. Such is the case when the sample contains a mixture of biological material from male and female individuals, as in mixed samples of blood with saliva or blood from two individuals. Because we cannot separate male from female cells (and their respective DNA) when no spermatozoa are present, we cannot tell which component is derived from the male and which is from the female. Another example is the case of a sexual assault in which the evidence contains a mixture of DNA, with one component originating from a male assailant and the other from a female victim. In situations like these, testing of sex-specific, Y-STR genetic markers (loci) can be very useful. This kind of testing can provide information exclusively about the male component in the mixture.

An additional consideration is the fact that mixtures of DNA from two sources can contain different amounts of material from each individual. Thus, the ratio of female DNA to male DNA in such a mixture may be 1:1 to 5:1 to 10:1, or even greater. When female DNA far exceeds (>10:1) the quantity of male

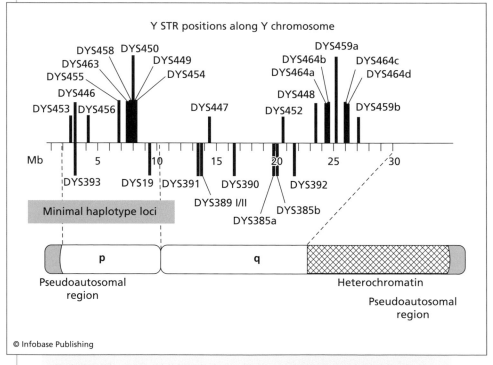

FIGURE 7.1 The Y chromosome STR loci are located primarily on the long arm (q) with the remainder on the short arm (p) of the chromosome. (Adapted from a graphic by Dr. John Butler of the National Institute of Standards and Technology with his permission.)

DNA in a mixture, autosomal STR typing will reflect only the female genetic profile; the male genetic profile will be masked. This is a result of the interactions of the PCR reagents at the molecular level and competition for template DNA during amplification. The DNA that is available in the greater quantity will be preferentially amplified and therefore preferentially genotyped. It is not unusual in rape cases to find that the female DNA far exceeds the amount of the attacker's DNA in some mixed evidence; as a result, the tests fail to reveal the male's genetic profile. In such cases, Y-STR typing is very helpful and is often used to supplement autosomal STR DNA testing. Y-STR typing can also be very informative when multiple assailants commit a rape. The results of Y-STR testing can reveal the number of assailants and provide valuable genetic information for identifying each one.

PATRILINEAL INHERITANCE

The Y chromosome and all of its genes are inherited paternally in a direct lineage from father, to son, to grandson, and so on. A male also shares the same Y chromosome genes with his brother, uncle, nephew, and cousin on his paternal side. With the exception of a mutation, these genes are passed unchanged from generation to generation. The STR loci on the Y chromosome are all linked and are therefore inherited together as a unit (Figure 7.1). Furthermore, because a male (having the X and Y sex chromosomes) has only one set of these Y markers, the genetic profile obtained from typing the Y-STR loci is a **haplotype**, consisting of only a single gene at each locus. One can therefore determine the haplotype of an individual at a number of loci on the Y chromosome. More than 100 such loci have been described, but far fewer have been validated; as a result, only a small fraction of them are usually typed.

MULTIPLEXES

It has been demonstrated that, with as little as 150 to 200 pico-grams of male DNA, 19 Y-STR loci can be successfully typed using 2 multiplex reactions: These loci are as follows:

Multiplex I–9 Loci

DYS393, DYS392, DYS391, DYS389I, DYS389II, DYS461, DYS438, DYS385a, and DYS385b.

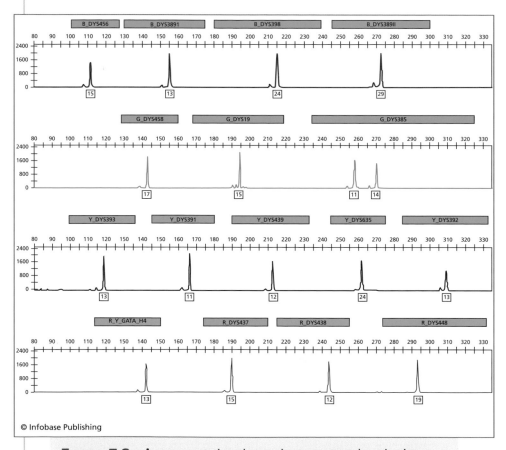

© Infobase Publishing

FIGURE 7.2 A representative electropherogram produced using the Yfiler™ kit is shown here. The four panels correspond to 6-FAM™, VIC®, NED™, and Pet® dye-labeled peaks. The haplotype is shown with the allele number displayed underneath each peak.

Multiplex II–10 Loci

DYS425, DYS388, DYS390, DYS439, DYS434, DYS437, Y-GATA-C.4, DYS460, Y-GATA-H.4, and DYS19.

Two small regions of the Y chromosome (constituting 5%) are homologous to the X chromosome, and therefore can undergo recombination. These recombining regions are located on the ends of the X and Y chromosomes (Figure 7.2). All of the 19 Y-STR loci listed on this page and the previous page are found on the nonrecombining region of the Y chromosome, so the genes at each of these loci are inherited intact from father to son, without alteration of sequence. As with autosomal STRs, the polymorphisms found at each Y-STR locus are based on length, not sequence differences. As a result, they can be analyzed using the same equipment (genetic sequencer) and techniques as are used for the 13 CODIS autosomal STRs. Furthermore, it has been demonstrated that, in male/female mixtures in ratios of up to 1:4,000, the male component (Y-STR profile) can still be detected. Validation studies have proven this system to be accurate, specific, sensitive, reliable, and reproducible. Also, because there is only one allele at each locus, the genotype is easy to interpret.

HAPLOTYPING

The one disadvantage in using Y-STR testing is that, because the loci are linked on the same chromosome, we cannot use the product rule to generate the extraordinary statistics that usually accompany autosomal STR typing. In the latter case, we can obtain the frequency of the combination of all the alleles by multiplying allele frequencies for each locus. In the former case, we cannot multiply frequencies because all Y-STR loci are inherited as a unit. We must use the "counting" method to determine frequencies of alleles on Y-STR loci. Thus, the power of discrimination is far lower for Y chromosome testing than it is for the autosomal STR loci.

Several commercial kits are now available for Y chromosome STR testing, including ReliaGene Technologies' Y-Plex™12, which permits testing of 11 Y-STR loci plus amelogenin; Promega Corporation's Powerplex Y multiplex kit, which permits testing of 12 loci; and Applied Biosystems' Y-Filer kit, which permits testing of 17 STR loci.

In addition to sexual assault cases, Y chromosome STR testing has been used in immigration cases to prove blood relationships. It can also be used in anthropological studies to follow population migration patterns over vast periods of time and determine relationships between populations that have become separated and distinct over time, and, of course, in paternity casework in which the circumstances of the situation may require Y-STR analysis. Y-STR chromosome databases can be found at http://www.ystr.org. Another important database Web site is http://www.yhrd.org (Y-Chromosome Haplotype Reference Database). Finally, a Web site that provides extensive information on the subject of Y-STRs is http://www.cstl.nist.gov/biotech/strbase/y_strs.htm.

There is also interest in the scientific community in developing multiplex procedures to study Y chromosome **Single Nucleotide Polymorphisms (SNPs)**. Each of these SNP sites is a **biallelic** marker (G>A, G>C, C>T, A>C, etc.). The genetic profile of an individual based on SNPs is classified as a **haplogroup** rather than a haplotype as described previously. In 2002, the Y Chromosome Consortium described a "YCC Tree," which details approximately 250 biallelic markers, thereby differentiating 153 different haplogroups. This area of research promises to introduce another important method that can be applied to human identification and perhaps will be useful in determining the ethnicity of a DNA donor.

Frequency and Probability

Forensic DNA evidence serves the cause of justice when it proves that an incorrectly accused person is innocent of a crime or links a suspect to a victim or a crime scene. If the genotype of the evidence sample differs from that of the suspect's exemplar (reference sample), the suspect is excluded or eliminated as a potential donor of the evidence. Should the genotypes of the suspect and evidence match, the suspect is included, that is, he or she cannot be eliminated as the donor.

The discussion up to this point has concentrated on how to establish that a match exists between the genetic profile of a suspect and the evidence of a crime. Before rushing to convict, however, a crucial question remains to be answered: "Is there some other person whose genetic profile is identical to that of the suspect?" Quite clearly, the existence of an identical sibling (twin or triplet, for example) is such a situation. In certain cases, this has led to an insolvable situation in which one cannot determine from whom the evidentiary DNA originated. Putting aside this possibility, a related question remains: "Does a person without an identical sibling have a genetic profile that matches some other individual?"

First, it is important to note that, when one deals with the chance (probability) that two genetic profiles will be identical, it is not possible to come to a conclusion with absolute certainty. The best that can be achieved is a claim of virtual certainty, based on the extremely small probability of identical genetic profiles occurring.

It is also important to realize that the probability of finding an identical genetic profile in a population depends completely on the incidence (frequency) of the genetic profile in the same population. If, for example, a genetic profile has an estimated frequency of one in a million in a population, then it is a million times more likely that the next person examined, identical siblings excluded, will have a different genetic profile. Under these conditions, it is quite clear that the size of the population is critical in deciding whether one can state with "virtual certainty" that the genetic profile under investigation is unique to a particular suspect.

SUBPOPULATIONS

Another question remains to be answered, namely, "To which population does a particular individual belong?" The world population consists of many groups of people, some of whom can trace their origin to a particular continent: Africa, Asia, or Europe, for example. Complicating the situation are marriages, in both ancient and modern times, between members of these various groups. Especially in a country such as the United States, which is populated by people from all parts of the world, it is sometimes very difficult to establish the population or populations from which an individual originates. In setting up CODIS, the FBI listed five large ethnic groups: (1) African American, (2) Asian American, (3) European American, (4) Southeastern Hispanic, and (5) Southwestern Hispanic.

For the sake of simplicity, the present analysis is restricted to an example from the European-American population. The two most frequent alleles of the STR D3S1358 and their frequencies are (1) 15 (0.246) and (2) 16 (0.232). What is the expected (probable) frequency of a 15,16 heterozygote in the population? The answer is obtained by multiplying 0.246 by 0.232 by 2. One can easily see that, in order to get the probability (expected frequency) of a heterozygote in a population, you need to multiply the frequencies of the two alleles that form the heterozygote, but why double this number? Doubling the number is required because there are two ways to form a heterozygote. In the present example, a heterozygote can be formed if the 15 allele comes with the sperm, and the 16 allele comes with the egg, or the reverse situation. This doubles the chance of a D3S1358 15,16 heterozygote being formed, giving us a probability of finding this genotype in the European-American population of 0.114. That is, approximately 11 to 12 such individuals in a randomly chosen group of 100 unrelated persons would have this genotype. Worded somewhat differently, approximately 11% of the European-American population are 15,16 heterozygotes for D3S1358.

To carry the analysis one step further: In the European-American population, the most frequent allele of STR-VWA and its frequency are 17 (0.263). What is the probable frequency of a 17,17 homozygote (usually indicated by a single number 17) in the population? Clearly, only one set of circumstances will result in the formation of a homozygote, namely, both egg and sperm must contain the same allele. The chance of this occurring in the European-American population is 0.069 (0.263 x 0.263), or about 7 such individuals in a group of 100 unrelated persons.

THE PRODUCT RULE

The next step in determining the **random match probability (RMP)** of a genetic profile is to calculate the chance of finding an individual in this population who is both D3S1358 15,16 and

VWA 17. If the STRs are inherited independently of each other, as are all the CODIS STRs, the chance of both genotypes occurring in the same individual becomes the product of the probabilities of each occurring alone. This is known as the product rule. In the present case, it is obtained by multiplying 0.114 by 0.069. The answer is 0.00787, or about 8 persons in a group of 1,000 individuals.

At this stage, it is important to ask the overall question: What is the probability of a random match in the European-American population that will include all the most frequent genotypes of the CODIS STRs? One finds that the total match probability of the most frequently occurring profile is 1 in 100 trillion. When we compare 100 trillion to the somewhat more than 6 billion individuals on Earth, we undoubtedly have a case of *virtual certainty* that no one on this planet has this genetic profile. The same can be said for any other independently formed genetic profile in this population. It must also be pointed out that comparable calculations involving the other FBI-designated population groups give similar results.

PATERNITY TESTING

Another forensic problem whose solution can be achieved by analyzing DNA evidence is disputed paternity. A report by the American Association of Blood Banks states that, of the tests performed to establish paternity, 28% show that the mother's husband is not the child's biological father. This, of course, does not mean that 28% of the children born in the United States are illegitimate. It does indicate, however, that in a significant percentage of troubled marriages, extramarital affairs do occur. In addition, there is the all-too-common occurrence, after the death of a wealthy man, of one or more individuals claiming to be the illegitimate children of the deceased and therefore entitled to part or all of his estate. In many such cases, the mothers of the "revealed children" are prepared to testify that they were seduced by the now-deceased. The need for **paternity testing** has become so great that it has spawned a new service industry.

Consider the following case of disputed paternity: A test of FBI CODIS STR D5S818 shows that a mother, child, and husband are all 11,11 homozygotes. The population frequency of the 11 allele is 0.410. On the surface, there appears to be no reason to doubt the paternity of the child. Because of the nature of the marital situation, however, the possibility is raised that the 11-carrying sperm came from some other male (referred to as a *random male.*) A statistical solution takes the form of what is called a **Paternity Index** (PI).

The PI is actually a ratio of two numbers. The numerator, traditionally designated by the letter "X," is the probability that the genotype of any section of a child's DNA, such as an STR, is formed by a combination of homologous alleles from the child's mother and her husband. The denominator, labeled "Y," is the likelihood that the child's genotype was formed by homologous alleles from the child's mother and a random male from the husband's population.

In calculating the PI, the chance that the mother was the source of the maternally inherited allele is "0.5" if she is a heterozygote and "1.0" if she is a homozygote for the allele in question. The same probabilities will apply for the paternally inherited allele, when calculating "X," in the case of the mother's husband. In calculating the "Y," however, the likelihood of a random male being the source of the paternally inherited allele will be the population frequency of the allele. For a random male, there can be no question of zygosity because he is an unknown person.

What has been outlined for the preceding marital situation also applies to a case in which an unmarried female identifies a particular male as the biological father of her child. In laboratory reports and court records, it is customary to designate both the mother's husband (H) and the random male (RM) as the **alleged father** (AF).

As an aid in determining paternity, the American Association of Blood Banks has prepared a table (Table 8.1) showing:

- the genotypes of the individuals comprising the various types of trios [mother (M), child (C), alleged father (AF)],

- the corresponding values of X and Y for each type of trio, and

- the formula for calculating the PI for each type of trio.

To better understand how Table 8.1 was constructed, let us analyze the marital situation described earlier, which corresponds to case #1 in Table 8.1. From the data presented, we get the following PI= X/Y = (M × H) / (M × RM) = (1 × 1) / (1 × 0.410) = 1/0.410 = 2.44.

Table 8.1 **Paternity Index Formulas For Various Trios**

Case#	M (Mother)	C (Child)	AF (Alleged Father)	X	Y	PI (X / Y)
1	AA	AA	AA	1	a	1 / a
2	AB	AB	AB	0.5	0.5 (a+b)	1 / (a+b)
3	AB	AB	AC	0.25	0.5 (a+b)	1 / [2(a+b)]
4	AB	AB	AA	0.5	0.5 (a+b)	1 / (a+b)
5	BD	AB	AC	0.25	0.5a	1 / 2a

The question comes up: "What does the PI actually tell us about the probability that the husband is the biological father of the child?" By itself, the PI is not in a familiar form to answer the question. To obtain a generally understandable answer, we must calculate the *probability of paternity* (POP), which is

$$POP = PI/(PI + 1)$$

In the present case, this becomes

$$POP = 2.44/(2.44 + 1) = 2.44/3.44 = 70.9\%$$

This states that there is a 70.9% chance that the husband is the biological father.

Clearly, the next question is: "Is this sufficient for the court to declare that the husband is the father?" The answer is "no." We must, therefore, continue our analysis.

Consider the distribution of alleles of STR D8S1179: The mother is found to be 13,15, the child is 13,15, and the husband is 13,15. The population frequency of the 13 allele, labeled "a," is 0.326; that of the 15 allele, labeled "b," is 0.106. This situation corresponds to case #2 in Table 8.1. Again, on the surface there appears to be no problem. The question remains, however, "What is the mathematical support that the husband is the father?" Here, the PI is as follows:

$$PI = X/Y = (M \times H)(2)/[M \times (a+b)] =$$
$$(.5 \times .5)(2)/[.5 \times (.326 + .106)] = 2.31$$

On the surface, this formula raises certain questions. Why, in calculating X, must one multiply $(M \times H)$ by 2? Why, in calculating Y must one include population frequencies of both alleles? With respect to the X factor, one must consider the fact that all members of the family trio are identical heterozygotes.

As a result, there are two ways that the mother and her husband's alleles can combine to form the child's genotype. This possibility is taken into account by multiplying the numerator by 2. In similar fashion for Y, one must take into account that a random male carrying either allele could serve as biological father, providing the mother contributed the corresponding heterozygote-forming allele. It should be noted that, in Table 8.1, cases 2, 3, and 4 all deal with situations involving identical heterozygous genotypes of mother and child, and all have the (a + b) component in the Y factor.

As was done for a situation involving two independent probabilities, we can multiply this PI by that obtained for D5S818 to get the cumulative probability of the two events occurring simultaneously (product rule). In the present case, the use of the product rule provides the **Cumulative Paternity Index (CPI).** The product is 5.64, making the POP 84.94% that the husband is the biological father.

Again we must ask if this is sufficient to establish the husband as the father. This time the answer is, "not yet." To feel confident about their rulings on paternity, the courts require a POP of at least 99.0%. This is achieved when the CPI reaches a value of 99. In the present case, the data on VWA supply the necessary assurance. The mother is found to be 13,15, the child is 13,20, and the husband is 14,20. The population frequency of the 20 allele is 0.016. This situation corresponds to case #5 in Table 8.1. The PI is calculated to be 31.25. Applying the product rule, we obtain CPI of 176.25 and a POP of 99.44%. This POP value, in effect, says there is less than a 1% chance that a random male could be the child's biological father.

The Future of DNA Analysis

Forensic DNA analysis is a rapidly progressing field, and new instrumentation and new techniques are constantly being developed. Most of the current advances in DNA analysis instrumentation involve increasing the number of samples that can be processed at once (throughput) and/or decreasing the size of the instruments that are used.

Many states are broadening the categories of offender reference samples that will be put into DNA databases. Initially only profiles from those who had committed violent crimes were entered, but sampling in some states has been extended to include all felonies and misdemeanors, and in some cases even arrestees. In addition to this increased number of categories and therefore total number of new samples, there is still a backlog of samples already taken from convicted offenders that are yet to be extracted, analyzed, and uploaded into the database.

To help speed up the analysis of these reference samples, robotic instruments that automate DNA extraction and processing are being developed, and some are already in use in high-throughput laboratories. In addition, instruments and procedures are also being developed to speed up the DNA typing process through faster analysis and/or analysis of many more samples at once. Instruments of this type include multicapillary CE instruments that are currently in use in many high-through-put laboratories.

Another important area of instrument development involves attempts to create portable instruments to analyze biological evidence right at the crime scene by miniaturizing the forensic DNA analysis equipment. Such devices could also be used to produce faster, less expensive ways of analyzing DNA samples in the laboratory. Instruments being developed for these purposes include miniature **thermal cyclers** for PCR and small microchip capillary electrophoresis devices for DNA analysis.

NEW TECHNIQUES FOR FORENSIC DNA ANALYSIS

Although other methods of DNA profiling are being investigated and developed, STR analysis will probably remain the major means of DNA typing for many years to come. As of March 2006, the National DNA Index System (NDIS) portion of the FBI CODIS database contained more than 3 million profiles from convicted offenders and more than 134,000 forensic profiles. Since the bulk of the identification information already available in the CODIS database and other DNA databases throughout the world is in the form of STR profiles, all the reference and forensic evidence samples in the databases would have to be reanalyzed if the types of DNA profiles to be uploaded were changed. For this reason, most of the new techniques being developed are aimed at improving STR analysis when the DNA is present in only very small amounts or has been severely degraded. Other new methodologies are also being used to compliment STR analysis, especially in cases in which full STR profiles cannot be obtained.

LOW COPY NUMBER (LCN) DNA

Forensic DNA analysis techniques have become more sensitive and discriminating in recent years. Most of the commercial kits available for traditional STR analysis, however, will work well only when DNA samples contain anywhere from 0.5 to 2 nanograms of DNA. At these DNA concentrations, all of the STR alleles in the sample can be amplified by PCR and analyzed to obtain a full DNA profile.

Most blood or semen stains recovered from violent crime scenes contain more than enough DNA for traditional STR analysis. If DNA profiling could be done on samples that contained much less DNA, however, then many more evidence samples would be analyzed, and many more nonviolent crime investigations might be solved with DNA profiling.

DNA that is present in a very small amount (less than 100 pg) is known as **low copy number (LCN)** DNA. Since there are about 6 pg of DNA in a typical human diploid cell, an LCN sample would therefore contain less than 17 cells. To be able to analyze samples containing LCN amounts of DNA, the sensitivity of the assay must be increased. This is usually done by increasing the number of PCR cycles from the 28 or 30 suggested for commercial kits to about 34 cycles. With increased cycles of PCR, very small starting amounts of DNA may be analyzed.

Numerous problems can arise with LCN DNA analysis, and many of these may interfere with the interpretation of LCN DNA profiles. Because so little DNA is present in an LCN DNA sample, less than a full compliment of the genome may be available for amplification. In addition, because only the loci that are amplified in the first rounds of PCR will probably show up in the final DNA profile, repeated amplifications of the same LCN sample may give different results. This phenomenon, known as stochastic variation, frequently occurs with LCN DNA analysis. Sometimes only one of the two alleles of a heterozygous STR locus will be amplified (allele dropout), and the locus mistakenly appears in the profile as homozygous. Other times, an entire STR locus may fail to amplify (locus dropout) or extra alleles may appear (allele drop in). Because of the stochastic variation of these amplification artifacts, LCN DNA samples are usually amplified three times, and the only alleles reported are those that are present in at least two of the three profiles produced from the same sample.

Additional complications occur with LCN DNA because the smaller amount of input DNA and the increased sensitivity of the PCR amplification make contamination artifacts (allele drop in) more likely. It is also possible that the DNA present in the original LCN DNA sample is not connected to the crime under investigation. For example, it may have come into the evidence sample by secondary transfer (for example, from individuals the offender had contact with before touching the evidence), or from other individuals who may have touched the item before the evidence was collected.

Although LCN DNA analysis is not yet used in U.S. courts, many laboratories are beginning to analyze material with less DNA for leads in burglary cases. In England, where LCN DNA analysis was pioneered, DNA profiles have also been successfully generated from items such as discarded tools, matchsticks, and weapon handles.

MINI-STRS AND MINIPLEXES

In some instances, the DNA template to be used for forensic DNA analysis of STRs may have become highly degraded. This type of degradation can be caused by bacteria present in the sample, or through oxidative or biochemical processes. Commercial STR multiplex kits produce PCR products that range in size from about 100 to 480 bp. When the DNA template is highly

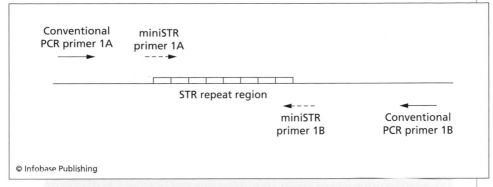

Conventional
PCR primer 1A

miniSTR
primer 1A

STR repeat region

miniSTR
primer 1B

Conventional
PCR primer 1B

© Infobase Publishing

FIGURE 9.1   MiniSTRs are produced by performing the PCR reaction using primers that are designed to hybridize to a single-stranded DNA template closer to the target core repeat region than normal STR primers.

degraded, the larger STRs are usually not amplified, and only a partial profile can be obtained. Some of the newer techniques that have been developed for forensic DNA typing aid in the analysis of highly degraded DNA.

MiniSTRs, which produce reduced-size STR **amplicons**, were developed and used to analyze the degraded DNA from victims of the World Trade Center disaster. The primers for miniSTRs were created by moving the primer binding regions as close as possible to the repeat region of an STR, so that the amplicons produced by PCR can be much smaller than those produced with traditional STR primers (Figure 9.1). Multiplex miniSTRs (**miniplexes**) have been shown to produce full STR profiles with degraded DNA samples that gave only partial profiles with traditional primers, and they have recently been shown to give fuller profiles with LCN DNA samples as well. Since primer positions can be altered to produce miniSTRs for most CODIS loci, most of the information already present in DNA databases would still be useable if STR analysis were eventually changed to a miniplex format.

SINGLE NUCLEOTIDE POLYMORPHISMS (SNPS)

STR typing of autosomal loci will probably continue as the preferred method of DNA profiling for many years. Additional DNA markers are frequently used, however, to obtain more information about a particular sample.

Another type of DNA analysis that is being developed for both autosomes and Y chromosomes involves the typing of single nucleotide polymorphisms (SNPs). An SNP is defined as a single base difference between individuals at a particular point in the genome. The human genome contains millions of SNPs, and some have been used as markers in medical studies to track genetic diseases. In forensics, SNPs are being used together with STR analysis, especially in cases in which a complete STR profile cannot be obtained from a DNA sample, a phenomenon that is common when DNA is highly degraded. (Both SNP and miniSTR analysis were used to help identify World Trade Center disaster victims.)

Although most of the variable regions of STRs used for DNA profiling are composed of multiples of a four-nucleotide repeat, an SNP involves only one differing nucleotide. PCR products from SNPs can therefore be much smaller than those of STRs. SNPs are not as informative as STRs because there are usually only two possible nucleotides for a SNP; more than five variations in the number of repeated tetranucleotides can be found at most STR loci. Because of this, many more SNP markers would have to be analyzed to get the same power of discrimination provided by the 13 CODIS STRs. Because SNPs have a lower mutation rate than STRs, however, and are thus more likely to become fixed in a population, SNPs may be potentially useful in predicting the ethnic origin of an offender.

SNP analysis is frequently done by minisequencing to identify the nucleotide that has been changed. Minisequencing is a variation of the typical DNA sequencing method used for mtDNA analysis (described in Chapter 4). In minisequencing, the SNP and the DNA region immediately surrounding it are amplified; this PCR product is then used in a PCR reaction in which only one new nucleotide, the one that defines the SNP, is added after the primer binds. This is accomplished by using only the type of nucleotide (ddNTP) that stops amplification once it is added. The four different ddNTPs are each labeled with a different fluorescent dye, so that the nucleotide present in the SNP can be identified. Fortunately, SNP analysis can also be performed as a multiplex allowing many SNPs to be identified simultaneously.

Other assays being developed and used to detect SNPs involve variations of techniques used in DNA **microarrays**. These **arrays** contain a large number of single-stranded DNA fragments (probes) that represent the SNPs (or other markers or genes of interest), and these are attached to a matrix or membrane in a known position in a tightly spaced grid (microarray) or linear pattern (linear array). The regions of interest are labeled with biotin during amplification of the DNA sample (many SNPs can be amplified at once), and the labeled PCR product is then hybridized to the array. Only DNA that is complementary to the probe will bind to the array and be detectable after washing. By examining which positions on the array are labeled, one can determine the sequences (or SNPs) present in the original DNA sample. A commercial typing kit is now available from Roche Applied Sciences. It permits detection of 18 SNPs within the HV1 and HV2 regions of mtDNA.

MATRIX-ASSISTED LASER DESORPTION-IONIZATION TIME-OF-FLIGHT MASS SPECTROMETRY (MALDI-TOF-MS)

MALDI-TOF-MS is a technique that is appropriate for high-throughput sample processing. Although it is not being used for STR typing, it has been shown to work for DNA analysis of STRs.

MALDI-TOF-MS is performed in a vacuum chamber, where the DNA is ionized, the ions separated by mass, and the charge-to-mass ratio determined. In addition to its speed (analysis in just seconds), this technique is highly accurate and reproducible. Rather than producing relative size measurements, such as those obtained from electrophoresis, MALDI-TOF-MS measures the actual molecular mass of a DNA fragment, so allelic ladders and sizing ladders are not necessary for accurate measurements. A problem with mass spectrometry is that both the sensitivity and resolution of the technique are reduced when the size of the DNA fragment is too large. Thus, to successfully analyze STRs, special primers closer to the repeat region than those used in traditional methods of STR analysis had to be designed. (The miniSTR primers that are being developed for analyzing degraded DNA might also be appropriate for MALDI-TOF DNA analysis.)

Because of its extreme speed, MALDI-TOF-MS has the potential for increasing the throughput of DNA samples to thousands per day. The high price of the equipment, however, (hundreds of thousands of dollars) and the general acceptance in courtrooms of the currently used methods for DNA typing make it unlikely that MS-based method will replace electrophoresis-based technologies for STR analysis.

GLOSSARY

Additions   Forms of mutation in which one or more nucleotide base(s) is (are) inserted within a DNA sequence.

Adenine   A purine base. It is one of the molecules present in nucleic acids, DNA and RNA. It is represented by the letter A.

Alleged father   One of the three people concerned in a paternity suit. The individual is purported to be the biological father of a child.

Allele   One of two or more alternative forms of a gene at a specific locus (chromosomal location).

Allelic ladder   A set of the most common genes for each locus being tested. It is used to determine sizes of unknown alleles based on comparison with those alleles found in the ladder.

Amelogenin   A locus found on the X and Y chromosome that determines gender. The alleles on these two chromosomes differ in size by four bases, with the Y allele being larger.

Amplicons   The DNA products of PCR amplification.

Amplification   The process of increasing the number of copies of a specific region of DNA by polymerase chain reaction.

Anode   A positive electrode in an electrophoretic system or battery.

Antiparallel   A term describing the opposite orientations of the two strands of a DNA double helix; the 5' end of one strand aligns with the 3' end of the other strand.

Arrays   Tools used to sift through and analyze the information contained within a genome. Microarrays consist of different nucleic acid probes that are chemically attached to a substrate, which can be a microchip, a glass slide, or a microsphere-sized bead.

Artifact   An inaccurate observation, effect, or result, especially one resulting from the technology used in scientific investigation or from experimental error.

Autosomes   Chromosomes other than the sex chromosomes X and Y. Humans have 22 pairs of autosomes.

Base pairs   Two complementary nucleotide bases held together by hydrogen bonds; base pairing occurs between A and T, and between G and C. It is also a unit (bp) of nucleic acid fragment length.

Biallelic   A polymorphic site on the human genome for which there are only two alleles, and that can usually be typed as one nucleotide base or another (G>A, G>C, C>T, A>C, etc.).

Cathode   A negative electrode in an electrophoretic system or battery.

Cell cycle   The cycle of cell growth, replication of the genetic material, and nuclear and cytoplasmic division.

Chelex 100   A resin composed of styrene divinylbenzene copolymers containing paired iminodiacetate ions, each of which acts as a chelating group. Used to extract DNA in single-stranded form from biological specimens. Chelex binds to polyvalent metal ions that would normally catalyze the breakdown of DNA at elevated temperatures in solutions with low ionic strength.

Chromosomes   The structures by which hereditary information, in the form of genes and noncoding DNA, is physically transmitted from one generation to the next; the structures within the cell nucleus that carry the genes.

Coding sequences   Arrangements of nucleotide bases in a region of DNA containing the information for the synthesis of a specific protein or ribonucleic acid.

CODIS   Combined DNA Index System, the national DNA database established in 1998 and containing genetic profiles obtained from felons as well as profiles obtained from crime scene evidence.

Codominance   A condition in which the phenotypes of both alleles of a particular gene are expressed equally in a heterozygote.

Cofiler   A PCR multiplex kit that can be used to provide genetic information at the following loci: CSF1PO, D16S539, THO1, TPOX, D3S1358, D7S820, and amelogenin.

Complementary base pairing   Bonding in which purine bases bond only with pyrimidine bases, thus, adenine can bind to thymine and guanine can bind to cytosine.

Control region (displacement loop or D-loop)   A segment of the mitochondrial genome that regulates replication of this DNA molecule. Because this region does not code for any genes, it has a high mutation rate and is the most polymorphic portion of the mitochondrial genome.

Control sample (positive and negative)   Every DNA test must include a sample that results in a known genetic profile to verify that the procedure is working properly. Similarly, an extraction negative sample and an amplification negative sample are included to verify that no contamination has occurred, which could interfere in interpretation of results.

Convicted offender database   A database within CODIS containing digitized genetic profiles obtained from individuals who have been convicted of eligible offenses, usually felonies. Some states are enacting legislation to include people who have been convicted of misdemeanors.

Counting method   A statistical approach to demonstrating the significance of a genetic profile when the product rule cannot be used (mtDNA sequencing and Y-STR haplotype analysis). The counting method must be used when alleles are not inherited independently from each other, as is the case in closely linked loci.

Crossing over   The breaking during meiosis of one maternal and one paternal chromosome, exchange of corresponding sections of DNA, and rejoining of the chromosomes. This process can result in an exchange of alleles between the chromosomes.

Cumulative Paternity Index   The combined paternity index calculated by multiplying the individual paternity indices obtained by testing multiple loci in the mother, child, and alleged father.

Cytosine   A pyrimidine base. It is one of the molecules present in nucleic acids DNA and RNA. It is represented by the letter C.

Degraded   Broken down, cleaved, or fragmented by chemical or physical means.

Deletions   Mutations involving a loss of one or more base pairs; the case in which a chromosomal segment, gene, or gene component is missing.

Deoxyribonucleic acid (DNA)   The genetic material of organisms. DNA is usually double stranded, composed of two complementary chains of nucleotides in the form of a double helix. The four chemical bases that make up DNA are adenine, cytosine, guanine, and thymine.

Deoxyribonucleotide triphosphate (dNTP)   One of four building blocks (monomers) used in the synthesis of a polynucleotide chain, such as DNA.

Dideoxyribonucleotide triphosphate (ddNTP)   A special type of nucleotide that stops the synthesis of DNA.

Dihybrids   Organisms heterozygous at two loci.

Diploid   Having two sets of chromosomes, in pairs (compare to haploid).

D-loop   Displacement loop; *see* **control region.**

Dominant   An allele whose phenotype is expressed in a heterozygote when present with a recessive allele; for example, "A" is dominant over "a" because the phenotypes of AA and Aa are the same.

Electrophoresis   A technique in which different molecules are separated by their rates of movement in an electric field.

Evidentiary database   One of the databases within CODIS that contains genetic profiles obtained from biological evidence left at crime scenes or obtained from victims.

Exclusion   The conclusion of DNA testing indicating that DNA obtained from evidence did not originate from the suspect (or victim).

Exemplar   A known specimen whose origin (suspect, victim, person, or persons to be eliminated) is established.

Extraction   Removal of DNA from cellular material through organic or inorganic methods; isolation or purification of DNA from proteins, carbohydrates, lipids, and other biochemicals present in cells.

Felonies   Serious crimes, as defined by statute or common law.

Fluorescence   Emission of light by a substance following excitation by higher-energy light. The emitted light always has a higher wavelength than the exciting light.

Fluorochrome   A dye with the capability of absorbing light energy of a specific wavelength and emitting light of a higher wavelength.

Gametes   Haploid reproductive cells; spermatozoa or ovum.

Genes   The basic units of heredity. Genes are sequences of DNA nucleotides on a chromosome that contain the information for the synthesis of a protein or RNA product; *see* **allele.**

Genome   All the genetic material in the chromosomes of a particular organism; its size is generally given as its total number of base pairs.

Genotype   The genetic makeup of an organism, as distinguished from its appearance or phenotype. It is expressed as the two alleles present at a single locus.

Guanine   A purine base; one of the molecules present in nucleic acids DNA and RNA. It is represented by the letter G.

Haplogroup   A large group of haplotypes; for example, Y chromosome haplogroups and mtDNA haplogroups. (In mtDNA, specific coding region and control region polymorphisms exist for each major ethnic population. Thus, variations can be grouped according to their existence in a specific population. Specific groups of haplotypes are observed to correspond to a specific ethnic population. In the Y chromosome, haplogroups are defined by many different biallelic markers that correspond to a number of major populations.)

Haploid   Having one set of chromosomes (compare *diploid*). The number of chromosomes found in gametes (sperm and egg).

Haplotype   A series of alleles (for different loci) located close together on the same chromosome that tend to be inherited together; the genetic constitution of an individual chromosome; a series of alleles at specific locations on a chromosome.

Heteroplasmy   The existence within an organism of genetic heterogeneity within the population of mitochondria.

Heterozygote   A diploid organism that carries different alleles at one or more genetic loci on its homologous chromosomes.

Homologous chromosomes   Chromosomes containing the same linear gene sequence but are derived from different parents.

Homozygote   A diploid organism that carries identical alleles at one or more genetic loci on its homologous chromosomes.

Hybridization   The reassociation of complementary strands of nucleic acids, nucleotides, or probes.

Hydrogen bonds   Weak bonds involving the sharing of an electron with a hydrogen atom; hydrogen bonds are important in the specificity of base pairing in nucleic acids and in determining protein shape.

Hypervariable region   A region of the mitochondrial genome that varies in nucleotide sequence from one individual to another; used to compare a suspect or victim with evidence when nuclear STR analysis cannot be successfully accomplished because of insufficient or degraded DNA.

Inclusion   Conclusion of DNA testing indicating that the suspect (or victim) cannot be excluded as a source of the DNA obtained from evidence; a DNA match over a significant number of loci.

Incomplete dominance   The situation in which both alleles of a heterozygote influence the phenotype. The phenotype is usually intermediate between the two homozygous phenotypes. The situation in which a heterozygote shows a phenotype somewhere (but not exactly halfway) intermediate between the corresponding homozygote phenotypes. (Exact intermediacy of phenotype is referred to as no dominance.)

Inconclusive   Report of results in which testing fails to indicate an inclusion, an exclusion, or a negative conclusion; Inability to conclude that a relationship exists between DNA obtained from the suspect or victim and evidence.

Independent assortment   The principle, discovered by Mendel, that genes on different chromosomes behave independently.

Locard's exchange principle   The concept that, when two objects come into contact, a physical exchange of matter occurs from one to the other.

Locus (pl. loci)   The specific physical location of a gene on a chromosome.

Low copy number   Less than 100 picograms of DNA isolated from a specimen requiring special cycling procedures to adequately amplify template DNA.

Meiosis   Cell division that produces gametes (or spores) with half the number of chromosomes of the parental cell.

Microarray (linear array)   An assay that can determine polymorphisms in the sequence of HV1 and HV2 regions of mtDNA. The commercial kit manufactured by Roche Applied Sciences tests for 18 SNPs using a system of 33 sequence-specific oligonucleotide (SSO) probes that are linearly bonded to a nylon membrane. Alternatively, arrays can be used to study genome expression.

Microvariants   Alleles that contain incomplete repeat units. Microvariants may or may not have the same size as the common alleles.

Miniplexes   Multiplex amplifications of miniSTRs.

MiniSTRs   Reduced-size STR PCR products created by using primers that bind more closely to the target region.

Misdemeanor   An offense less serious than a felony.

Mitochondrial DNA (mtDNA)   The circular double-stranded genome found within the mitochondria responsible for the production of various RNA products as well as specific proteins.

Mitochondria   DNA-containing eukaryotic organelles that are the site of ATP synthesis and cellular respiration.

Mitosis   Cell division that produces two daughter cells with nuclei identical to the parental cell.

Monohybrids   Organisms with heterozygous alleles at a single locus.

Glossary

Multiplex A laboratory approach that performs multiple sets of PCR reactions in parallel (simultaneously), greatly increasing speed and throughput while conserving evidence.

Mutation The original source of genetic variation caused, for example, by a change in a DNA base or a chromosome. Spontaneous mutations are those that appear without explanation; induced mutations are those attributed to a particular mutagenic agent.

Noncoding regions DNA that does not contain the information required to synthesize specific protein or RNA molecules; junk DNA.

Nucleic acid A nucleotide polymer; DNA and RNA.

Nuclein The term used by Friedrich Miescher to describe the substance present in cell nuclei, which he discovered in 1869 while examining bandages from wounded soldiers. Nuclein is DNA.

Nucleotides Units of nucleic acid composed of a phosphate, a five-carbon sugar (ribose or deoxyribose), and a nitrogen containing base (A, T, G, or C).

Nucleus The cellular organelle in eukaryotes that contains most of the genetic material.

Ovum The one functional product of every meiosis in female animals; egg cell.

Paternity Index Estimate of the likelihood that an alleged father is the biological father, compared to a randomly chosen, unrelated male (who is not being tested).

Paternity testing An analysis to determine the likelihood that an alleged father is actually the biological father, based on the genetic profiles of mother, child, and questioned individual.

Pedigree A family tree illustrating the inheritance of particular genotypes and/or phenotypes.

Phenotype The physical appearance or functional expression of a trait.

Polarity Directionality, referring to the fact that linear entities (for example, a single strand of DNA or RNA or a protein) have ends (5' and 3'; N and C) that differ from each other.

Polymerase   The enzyme responsible for synthesis of a polynucleotide chain, either DNA or RNA; the enzyme that adds poly(A) to mRNA, or to its precursor.

Polymerase chain reaction (PCR)   An in vitro process that yields millions of copies of desired DNA through repeated cycling of a reaction involving the enzyme DNA polymerase. Cycles include denaturation, annealing of primers, DNA polymerase-directed extension from primer binding sites, and ligation of all bases into a polymer.

Polymorphism   The existence of two or more genetically determined forms (alleles) in a population with substantial frequency. In practice, a polymorphic gene is one at which the frequency of the most common allele is less than 0.99.

Polynucleotide chain   A linear array of nucleotide bases held together by a backbone of sugar and phosphate molecules.

Power of discrimination   The ability of a test system (such as Profiler Plus or Cofiler) to distinguish two unrelated individuals. The higher the power of discrimination, the less likely that there will be a match between DNA from evidence and from a randomly selected individual. The power of discrimination is equal to 1/RMP, where RMP is the random match probability for the test system.

Primers (forward or reverse)   Small pieces of RNA or DNA that provide the free ends needed for DNA replication to begin.

Probability   The ratio of the frequency of a given event to the frequency of all possible events; the statistical chance that an event will take place.

Probes   Short segments of single-stranded DNA that are tagged with a chemically active group of atoms or with radioactive atoms and used to detect a particular complementary DNA sequence.

Product rule   The probability of two independent events occurring simultaneously, calculated as the multiplicand (product) of their independent probabilities.

Profiler Plus   A PCR multiplex kit that can be used to provide genetic information at the following nine loci D3S1358, VWA, FGA, D8S1179, D21S11, D18S51, D5S818, D13S317, and D7S820.

Pull-up peaks   Peaks that appear on an electropherogram as a result of spectral overlap (color bleeding from one spectral channel to another), resulting in what appears as additional smaller peaks of another color; usually occurs as a result of off-scale peaks and is also known as bleed through.

Purines   The larger of two kinds of bases found in DNA and RNA. A purine is a nitrogenous base with a double-ring structure, such as adenine (A) and guanine (G), (compare *pyrimidine*).

Pyrimidines   The smaller of two kinds of bases found in DNA and RNA. A pyrimidine is a nitrogenous base with a single-ring structure, such as cytosine (C), thymine (T), and uracil (U) (compare *purine*).

Random match probability (RMP)   The probability of finding a match of DNA obtained from two unrelated individuals in the relevant population. RMP = 1/power of discrimination.

Recessive   An allele or trait whose phenotype is not expressed in a heterozygote when a dominant allele is present; for example, "a" is recessive to "A" because the phenotype for Aa is like AA and not like aa.

Recombination   Process in which new combinations of maternal and paternal chromosomes, or parts of chromosomes, are formed in the gametes. Recombination occurs through crossing over and independent assortment.

Relative fluorescence units (RFUs)   A measure of the relative quantity of fluorescence emitted by a particular DNA fragment. Visually, the y axis on an electropherogram.

Restriction enzymes (endonucleases)   Proteins that cleave DNA molecules at particular base sequences.

Restriction fragment length polymorphism (RFLP)   Variation in the length of DNA fragments produced by a restriction endonuclease (restriction enzyme) that cuts at a polymorphic locus.

Ribonucleic acid (RNA)   A class of nucleic acids characterized by the presence of the sugar ribose and pyrimidine uracil, as opposed to the thymine of DNA.

Segregation   The principle, discovered by Mendel, that homologous chromosomes and their alleles separate during meiosis, thereby producing gametes with only one of the two alleles.

Sex chromosomes (X and Y chromosomes)   Chromosomes that determine gender and are present in different configurations in males (XY) and in females (XX).

Sex-linked   Describing a genetic characteristic, such as color blindness, that is determined by a gene on a sex chromosome and shows different patterns of inheritance in males and females. X-linked is a more specific term denoting a gene on the X chromosome.

Short tandem repeat (STR)   STRs consist of short repeat units, two to seven bases long, that are tandemly connected to each other, producing highly polymorphic loci. STRs usually are located in noncoding regions of DNA, either between genes or within introns.

Shoulder peaks   Peaks in an electropherogram that can occur when an allele is present with a second allele that differs by only a single base, such as in the case of the THO1 locus in which the alleles 9.3 and 10 are distinct and authentic alleles. Shoulder peaks can also occur when there is incomplete adenosine addition (adenylation) to some of the amplified products of PCR. As a result, you have DNA amplicons with or without an extra base.

Single nucleotide polymorphism (SNP)   A DNA sequence variation that occurs when a single nucleotide (adenine, thymine, cytosine, or guanine) in the genome sequence is altered.
See also *mutation, polymorphism*

Slot blot devices   Instruments used to quantify DNA. It incorporates a membrane on which DNA specimens are placed in a slotlike configuration, and concentrations of unknown DNA samples are compared to a set of calibrator DNA samples. A comparison of banding intensities is used to estimate the concentration of DNA in the unknown samples.

Somatic cells   The differentiated cells that make up the body tissues of multicellular plants and animals; all cells other than gametes or stem cells.

Spike   An electrical artifact that sometimes appears as a very sharp peak on an electropherogram and is easily differentiated from an authentic allele.

Stutter peak   An artifact observed in an electropherogram created by slippage during PCR amplification. A stutter peak is most often four bases to the left of a larger peak and is usually smaller than an authentic allele. Stutter peaks can create problems in interpreting mixtures because they can be confused with alleles from a minor contributor to a mixture.

Substrate control   A specimen obtained near an evidentiary stain or fluid found on a substrate (fabric, wood, or glass); it provides information helpful in interpreting the test results for the biological substance being examined.

Template DNA   The DNA that is put into the PCR reaction mix to be copied. This template DNA is first denatured by elevating the temperature and then annealed to the primers. The Taq polymerase extends the primers by directing dNTPs to position themselves in a complementary manner to the sequence of bases on the template.

Tetranucleotides   Four base pair repeat units.

Thermal cyclers   The computer-controlled instruments that regulate the temperature and length of time to which the amplification reagents (in microtubes) are exposed during the PCR amplification process. The instrument is set to perform a number of temperature shifts upward and downward, resulting in repeated replication of the template DNA.

Thymine   A pyrimidine base; one of the molecules present in the nucleic acid DNA. It is represented by the letter T.

Traits   Apparent distinguishing characteristics such as height, weight, eye color, and hair color.

Translation   The process in which the genetic code carried by mRNA directs the synthesis of proteins from amino acids.

True breeding   A group of identical individuals that always produce offspring of the same phenotype when intercrossed.

Variable number of tandem repeats (VNTR)   A polymorphic locus where alleles differ primarily in the number of times that a stretch of nucleotides (core repeat) is tandemly repeated. The size of the core differentiates the VNTR from the STR. The former is usually in the range of 15 to 30 bases long whereas the latter is in the range of 2 to 7 bases long.

Zygote   A diploid cell that results from the fusion of male and female gametes.

BIBLIOGRAPHY

Baechtel, F.S. "D1S80 Typing of DNA from Simulated Forensic Specimens." *Journal of Forensic Science* 40 (1995): pp. 536–545.

———. "The Identification of Semen Stains." In *Forensic Science Handbook,* Vol. 2, edited by Richard Saferstein. Englewood Cliffs, N.J.: Prentice Hall, 1988.

Blake, E., J. Mihalovich, R. Higuchi, P.S. Walsh, and H.A. Erlich. "Polymerase Chain Reaction (PCR) Amplification and Human Leukocyte Antigen (HLA)-DQ Alpha Oligonucleotide Typing on Biological Evidence Samples Casework Experience." *Journal of Forensic Science* 37 (1992): pp. 700–726.

Culliford, B. *The Examination and Typing of Bloodstains in the Crime Laboratory.* Washington, D.C.: U.S. Government Printing Office, 1971.

Graves, H.C.B., G.F. Sensabaugh, and E.T. Blake. "Postcoital Detection of a Male-Specific Semen Protein." *New England Journal of Medicine* 312 (1985): pp. 338.

Holt, C.L., M. Buoncristiani, J.M. Wallin, T. Nguyen, K.D. Lazaruk, and P.S. Walsh. "TWGDAM Validation of AmpFlSTR™ PCR Amplification Kits for Forensic Casework." *Journal of Forensic Science* 47 (2002): pp. 66–96.

Jeffreys, A.J., V. Wilson, and S.L. Thein. "Hypervariable 'Minisatellite' Regions in Human DNA." *Nature* 314 (1985): pp. 67–73.

———. "Individual Specific 'Fingerprint' of Human DNA." *Nature* 314 (1985): pp. 76–79.

Mullis, K. "The Unusual Origin of the Polymerase Chain Reaction." *Scientific American* (1990): pp. 56–65.

Sensabaugh, G.F., and E.T. Blake. "DNA Analysis in Biological Evidence Applications of the Polymerase Chain Reaction." In *Forensic Science Handbook,* Vol. 3, edited by Richard Saferstein. Englewood Cliffs, N.J.: Prentice Hall, 1993.

Shaler, R.C. "Modern Forensic Biology." In *Forensic Science Handbook,* 2nd ed., edited by Richard Saferstein. Englewood Cliffs, N.J.: Prentice Hall, 2001.

Southern, E.M. "Detection of Specific Sequences among DNA Fragments Separated by Gel Electrophoresis." *Journal of Molecular Biology* 98 (1975): pp. 503–517.

Urquhart, A., C.P. Kimpton, T.J. Downes, and P. Gill. "Variation in Short Tandem Repeat Sequences—A Survey of Twelve Microsatellite Loci for Use as Forensic Identification Markers." *International Journal of Legal Medicine* 107 (1994): pp. 13–20.

Walsh, P.S., D.A. Metzger, and R. Higuchi. "Chelex 100 as a Medium for Simple Extraction of DNA for PCR-Based Typing from Forensic Material." *BioTechniques* 10 (1991): pp. 506–513.

Weber, J.L., and P.E. May. "Abundant Class of Human DNA Polymorphisms Which Can Be Typed Using the Polymerase Chain Reaction." *American Journal of Human Genetics* 44 (1989): pp. 388–396.

Wyman, A.R., and R. White. "A Highly Polymorphic Locus in Human DNA." *Proceedings of the National Academy of Sciences* 77 (1980): pp. 6754–6758.

FURTHER READING

Butler, J. M. *Forensic DNA Typing Biology and Technology Behind STR Markers,* 2nd ed. San Diego, Calif.: Elsevier Academic Press, 2005.

Inman, K. and N. Rudin. *An Introduction to Forensic DNA Analysis.* Boca Raton, Fla.: CRC Press, 2002.

Kobilinsky, L., T. Liotti, and J. Oeser-Sweat. *DNA: Forensic and Legal Applications.* Hoboken, N.J.: John Wiley & Sons, 2005.

Lee, H., and F. Tirnady. *Blood Evidence: How DNA Is Revolutionizing the Way We Solve Crimes.* Cambridge, Mass.: Perseus Publishing, 2003.

Web Sites

Advancing Justice Through DNA Technology

http://usdoj.gov/ag/dnapolicybook_cov.htm

American Academy of Forensic Sciences

http://www.aafs.org

DNA Testing: An Introduction for Non-Scientists

http://www.scientific.org/tutorials/articles/riley/riley.html

National Institute of Standards and Technology, Short Tandem Repeat DNA Internet Database

http://www.cstl.nist.gov/biotech/strbase/

National Law Enforcement Summit on DNA Technology

http://www.ojp.usdoj.gov/nij/topics/forensics/events/dnasummit/trans-2.html

Presidents DNA Initiative Advancing Justice Through DNA Technology

http://www.usdoj.gov/ovw/President_dna.htm

Principles of Forensic DNA for Officers of the Court

http://www.dna.gov/training/otc

PICTURE CREDITS

INDEX

Index

ABOUT THE AUTHORS

Lawrence Kobilinsky, Ph.D., is a professor of biology and immunology at The City University of New York John Jay College of Criminal Justice. He currently serves as science advisor to the college's president and is also a member of the doctoral faculties of biochemistry and criminal justice of the CUNY Graduate Center. He is an advisor to forensic laboratories around the world and serves as a consultant to attorneys on major crime issues related to DNA analysis and crime scene investigation.

Louis Levine, Ph.D., was a specialist in forensic genetics consulting who participated in more than 80 cases during his distinguished career. He was an expert panel member of the Assigned Counsel Plan of the city of New York and was consulted in cases by the Office of the Public Defender of Maryland and New Jersey as well as by the Innocence Project at the Benjamin N. Cardozo School of Law of Yeshiva University.

Henrietta Margolis-Nunno, Ph.D., J.D., is an assistant professor of biology at The City University of New York (CUNY) John Jay College of Criminal Justice, where she does research in the field of forensic DNA analysis. She received a Ph.D. from the CUNY Graduate Center and a J.D. from the Benjamin N. Cardozo School of Law, where she worked on the Innocence Project and in the Criminal Law Clinic.